AF577439

ART DECO

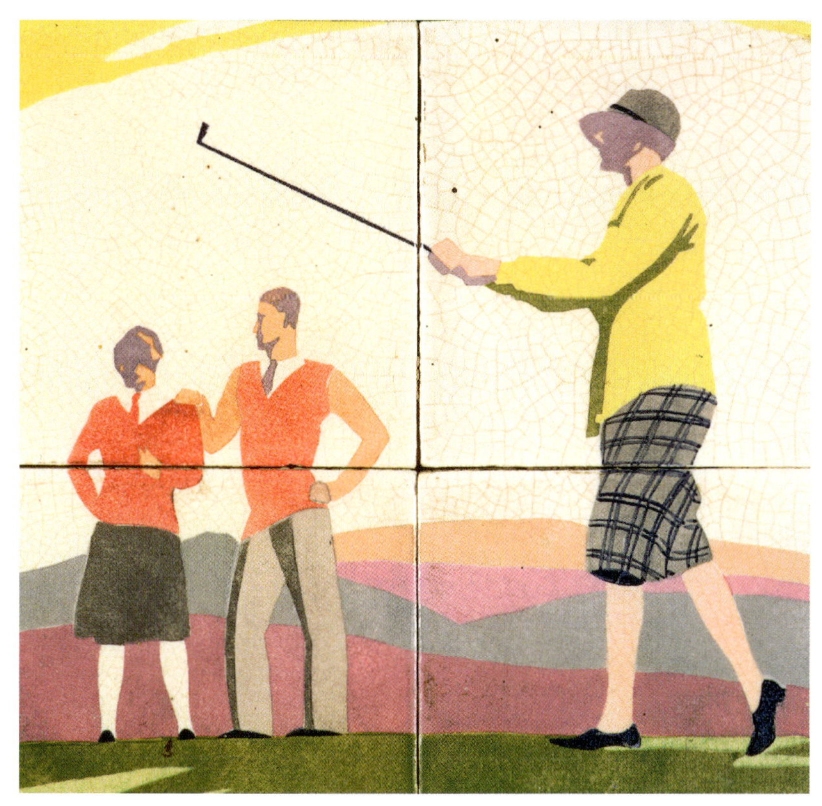

Published by Pulteney Press
1 Riverside Court
St Johns Road
Bath BA2 6PD

ISBN 978-1-906734-63-3

10 9 8 7 6 5 4 3 2 1

Designed and Produced by Omnipress Limited, UK

Printed in Indonesia

Photographs were kindly supplied by Bridgeman Art Library, London.
Picture research: Alex Edouard

Cover image: The Guggenheim Museum, New York, designed by Frank Lloyd Wright, 1943-1959.

ART DECO

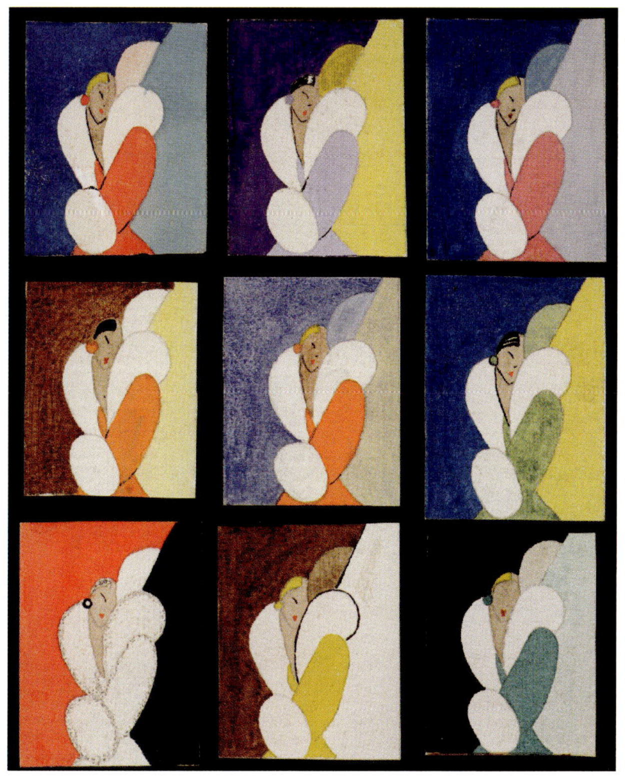

GORDON KERR

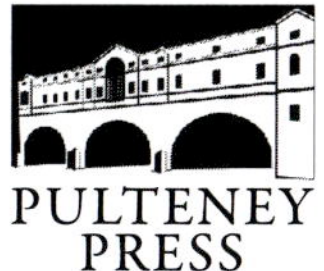

PULTENEY
PRESS

Contents

Contents

INTRODUCTION

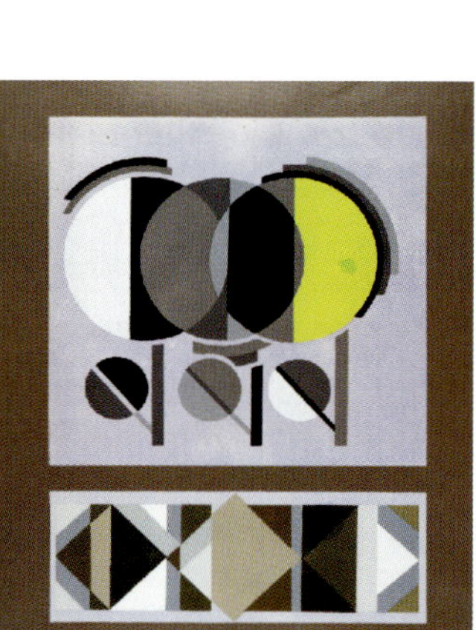

ILLUSTRATION FOR PLATE 10 OF *RELAIS* (RELAY)
Edouard Benedictus, 1930. Published by Calmann & King, London.

IT WAS NOT until long after its heyday that the name Art Deco became the common description for the popular international design movement that lasted from around 1925 until 1939 and the outbreak of the Second World War. Art Deco was originally called Style Moderne, amongst other things, and it was an exhibition curator, Bevis Hillier, who coined the term in a 1968 book about an exhibition he was putting on at the Minneapolis Institute of Arts. Not only did it have a name, but from that moment, Art Deco took off.

However, it should not surprise us too much that Art Deco was confusingly titled because, as a movement, it is hard to pin down, especially at the edges of the style. On many occasions it overlapped with other artistic trends of the first half of the twentieth century.

In the late 1800s and early 1900s, Art Nouveau had begun breaking down the barriers between art, architecture and the applied arts. It had united the arts in the way that thinkers such as John Ruskin had advocated, creating a pleasingly unified approach to a design movement, even if it varied in approach and even name, in individual countries. Art Deco, however, would finally blow the distinction between the arts aside, in what was probably its greatest and most lasting contribution to modern culture.

While Art Deco learned its lessons from Art Nouveau, it achieved its objectives using different techniques and stylistic devices. Art Deco was an amalgam of many different styles and movements that had exerted an influence on early twentieth-century art – Bauhaus, Futurism, the Neoclassical, Constructivism, Cubism, Modernism as well as Art Nouveau. Artists and craftspeople of all kinds were excited by this new movement – designers, architects, jewellers, sculptors, furniture makers, textile designers and many others. The result was that good design became available to ordinary people for the first time and was no longer merely the privilege of the rich, although Art Deco did provide much for them in the way of exquisitely crafted and designed luxury items.

There was no great hidden depths to Art Deco. It was as if art had to take exactly the opposite direction to the prevailing style of much of the work that was produced in the nineteenth century – historicism, the allegorical and classical mythology. Art Deco was without philosophical meaning; it was, as the name implies, simply decorative. It was also functional – something that could not be consistently claimed for Art Nouveau – modern and, above all, elegant.

The Paris Exposition Universelle of 1900 – a kind of World's Fair – had been a defining moment for Art Nouveau, providing artists and dealers with an opportunity to put the work of the new, modern style on display. More importantly, perhaps, it was also an opportunity to find a market for the work of Art Nouveau practitioners.

Following the exhibition's success, a group of French artists, amongst them Hector Guimard, Raoul Lachenal, Paul Follot, Maurice Dufrene and Eugène Grasset, formed a collective, under the name La Société des Artistes Décorateurs (the Society of Decorative Artists) with the intention of demonstrating to the world the quality of French decorative art, their aim being to prove that it was the best in the world. A grand exhibition was planned, but was postponed by the imminent First World War and it was not until 1925 that it eventually took place. The Exposition Internationale des Arts Décoratifs et Industriels Modernes (the International Exhibition of Modern Decorative and Industrial Art) was an opportunity to showcase French artists and designers and to find a market for their work. It was also a chance for French luxury goods manufacturers to catch up on competitors, especially the Germans, who were producing cheaper goods than the French.

The focus of the exhibition was resolutely modern, chiming perfectly with the frenetic post-war mood and the Jazz Age's pursuit of the quirky – the exotic, erotic and the esoteric – and not for nothing was '*Anything Goes*', one of the biggest hit songs of the time. Liberalism prevailed in all things – sex, speech and opinion. That applied also to art and design. Added to that was the fact that the people of Europe were tired of the austerity the First World War had enforced upon them, and the lavish opulence of Art Deco with its bright colours, its adventurous and accessible design and its sheer optimism about the future, was something of a relief.

While Art Nouveau was defined by its sinuous line and organic natural forms, Art

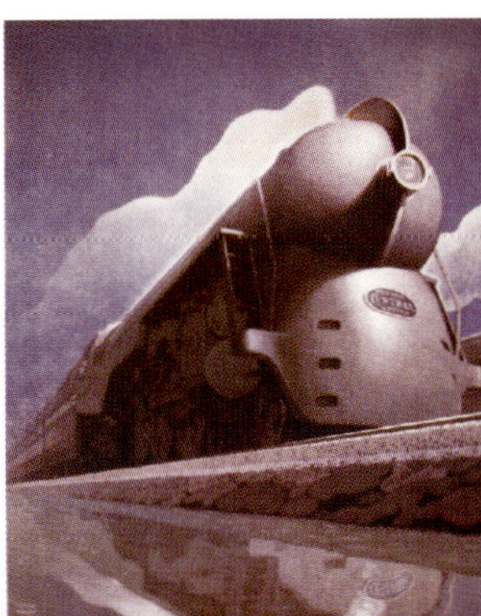

20TH CENTURY LIMITED

Poster advertising the new 16-hour train journey from New York to Chicago. Colour litho, by Leslie Ragan, 1938. Private collection.

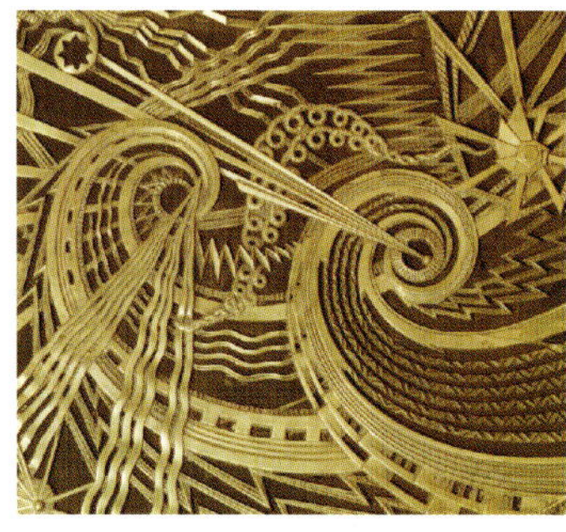

RADIATOR GRILL
For the Chanin Building, New York, USA, by Jacques Delamarre, c. 1929.

Deco was based on mathematical geometric shapes. The new and expanding fields of archeology, anthropology and ethnography provided surprising, but important influences and 'primitive' tribal art provided another impetus. Africa, ancient Egypt and the Aztecs of Mexico provided inspiration. Amidst global media coverage, Howard Carter had discovered the tomb of the Egyptian boy-king, Tutankhamun in 1922, and an exhibition of many of the items Carter found caused a sensation in Paris later that year. The ancient Egypt of the pharaohs was suddenly fashionable and artists and designers picked up on this and could even be said to have created the fashion.

The exciting new paraphernalia of the machine age also provided inspiration. The technology of streamlining, as had been developed for the new science of aviation and for trains, ocean-going liners and skyscrapers, also provided artists with inspiration. These influences can be clearly seen in many of the developing art styles around that time – in the faceted forms of decorative Cubism and Futurism.

Stepped forms, as found in the monoliths of Aztec Mexico and sweeping curves, indicating modernity and perhaps also speed, contrasted greatly with the interwoven lines of Art Nouveau and its gentler, more natural curves. Patterns of chevrons and trapezoids, zigzags and jigsaw shapes were characteristic of Art Deco and motifs such as the sunburst appeared everywhere. It can be seen on the spire of the Chrysler Building, designed by William van Alen in 1928 and also in Radio City Music Hall, designed in the early 1930s by Donald Deskey, the United States' foremost exponent of Art Deco. Slender, exotic animals appeared regularly – deer and greyhounds, for instance – and graceful, nude female figures, sometimes dancing, were common – as can be seen in Dimitri Chiparu's scuplture – 'Ayouta' – reflecting the new daring styles of dance as demonstrated by performers such Isadora Duncan. Above all, however, works of Art Deco were characterised by repeating geometric patterns, as evidenced in the work of the superb English ceramicist, Clarice Cliff.

Cliff was born in Stoke-on-Trent and her father was the great-great-great grandson of Thomas Wedgwood IV, who taught his younger brother Josiah the potter's art. Clarice worked in the potteries from the age of 13 and, being ambitious, learned all there was to know about ceramics. When she was given the opportunity to decorate some of the factory's defective whitewear, she did so by covering the flaws with simple patterns of brightly coloured triangles. It was a style that came to be known as 'Original Bizarre' and to everyone's surprise, it sold extremely well. Between 1928 and 1934, she introduced a style known as 'Fantasque', which depicted trees and cottages. Cliff went on to create numerous patterns of an Art Deco style that are eminently collectable today.

At the same time, materials used in Art Deco were exotic and original. Art Deco designers rejected traditional materials, choosing instead to work with more exotic and original materials. They liked the clean lines of aluminium and stainless steel, the cool elegance of marble, the luxurious feel of lacquered and inlaid wood and the sheer esoteric luxury of natural materials such as shark skin, known as shagreen, and zebra skin. Art Deco furniture was consequently expensive and affordable only for the well-off. Ebony, rare even in the 1920s, was much in evidence and parchment and snakeskin were used for decorative effect. Forged iron and chrome plated steel brought down the price and also exemplified the modernist objectives of Art Deco. The middle classes could afford this kind of furniture.

Furniture designer, Jacques-Emile Ruhlman's company, Ruhlman and Laurent, became one of the foremost interior design companies in France. Having first exhibited at the 1913 Salon d'Automne, Ruhlman refined his craft after the First World War to the point where his beautiful pieces, with tapering legs and perfect proportions, seemed to have been carved from one piece of wood – an extraordinary achievement and testament to the skill of his workmen.

Meanwhile, in Britain, Heal and Son and Gordon Russell were creating their own version of the modern style, more suited to the British market. Rather than the more exotic materials favoured by French designers, they made their furniture from familiar woods such as limed oak, walnut and chestnut, bringing out the natural beauty of the wood where possible, and using this to decorate the piece in question.

The development of technology played a big part in Art Deco's growth and popularity. In the 1930s, train stations in America were decorated in an Art Deco style because it said 'modern' to the traveller and reassured him or her about the journey ahead. Large ocean-going liners were the very embodiment of Art Deco. Vessels such as the *Normandie* and the *Queen Mary*

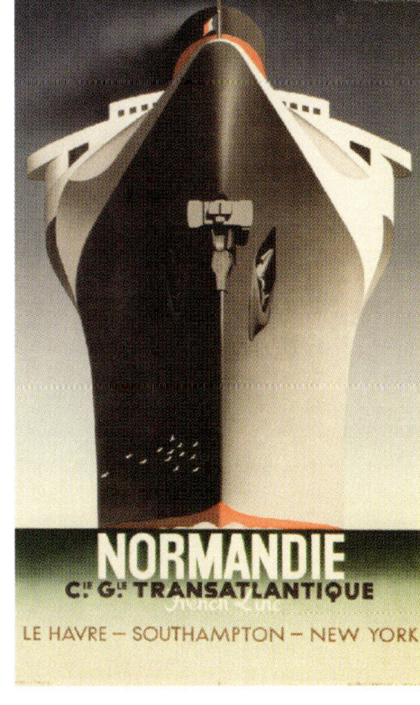

POSTER ADVERTISING TRANSATLANTIC FERRY CROSSINGS

Colour litho by Adolphe Jean-Marie Cassandre, printed by Alliance Graphique, Paris for Compagnie Generale Transatlantique, 1935. Private collection.

exploited the modernity of Art Deco in their interiors as well as in advertising material designed, in an age of competitiveness in crossing the Atlantic, to attract as much business as possible.

There was influence from the air, too. With the growth of the aviation industry and passenger-carrying planes, streamlining became an important science. The resultant aerodynamic designs also provided a wonderfully modern look to the machines whose high velocity required them – trains as well as aeroplanes. Art Deco welcomed these designs and this approach with enthusiasm and slipstreaming was applied to other objects that were part of everyday life, such as cars. Eventually, the slipstream look found its way into the design of objects that did not move at high velocities as well as objects that did not move at all, such as cigarette lighters, refrigerators and lamps, like the American, Walter Dorwin Teague's polaroid desk lamp.

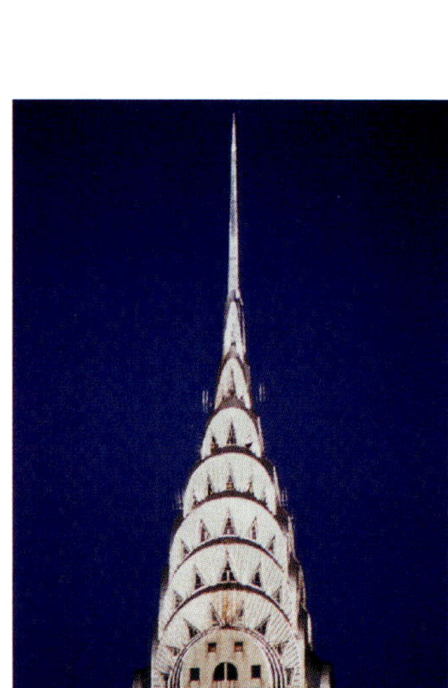

THE CHRYSLER BUILDING, NEW YORK, USA
designed by William van Alen, 1927-30.

For the first time, industrial designers were playing an important part in an art movement – men such as Walter Dorwin Teague, used the tenets of Art Deco in their work and produced objects that were functional and efficient, but were also, in effect, works of art. Other examples can be found in the work of the silversmith, Georg Jensen; furniture designer, Jean Dunand – an expert with lacquered wood; Edgar Brandt, who worked with wrought iron; Irish stained glass artist, Harry Clarke and Cartier, whose clocks and jewellery remain some of the world's most luxurious items. The development of exciting new materials such as plastic and bakelite were critical and confirmed artists in their belief that good design could be made inexpensive and, therefore, accessible to all through mass production.

A number of architects also embraced the Art Deco movement with unbridled enthusiasm, creating, especially in the United States, temples to the style. William van Alen's magnificent Art Deco masterpiece, the Chrysler Building, considered to be one of New York's finest buildings, is but one example. Even details such as the building's gargoyles follow Art Deco principles, modelled on Chrysler car accessories such as the bonnet ornaments of the Chrysler Plymouth, further exemplifying the machine age. Daniel H. Burnham Jr. et al's Chrysler Building at the Chicago World's Fair, 1933, a fair known as Century of Progress International Exposition, is another fine example of the Art Deco trend in architecture. Other architects of note who used the style included Raymond Hood, the architect responsible for the Rockefeller Centre in New York and the Tribune Tower in Chicago; Bruce Goff, who designed the Boston Avenue Methodist Church in Tulsa; Englishman Gilbert Scott; the Russian-English Joseph Sunlight; Albert Anis, who designed the Waldorf Towers Hotel in Chicago; Ralph Walker and Owen Williams – the appointed chief consulting civil engineer to the British Empire Exhibition, including Wembley Stadium, in 1923.

One of the most visible manifestations of Art Deco – even today – are the posters that were designed by a range of innovative graphic artists. Modern graphic design, decorating packaging, book jackets, CD covers and so on, can be said to have been born in the work of talented graphic artists such as A.M. Cassandre and Albert Staehle.

Art Deco lent itself particularly well to commercial uses, and A.M Cassandre, a Ukranian-French painter, poster artist and typeface designer, saw such potential in it that he set up his own advertising agency, calling it Alliance Graphique. He designed work for a range of clients during the 1930s, for one of whom, Dubonnet, he created the first posters specifically designed to be viewed by the occupants of fast-moving vehicles. One of his poster, for a cabinetmaker won first prize at the 1925 Exposition Internationale des Arts Décoratifs.

Talented painters and sculptors also formed an important part of the Art Deco movement. The exotic Tamara de Lempicka, whose life-story would fill several books, painted characteristically Art deco paintings whose roots can be seen in Cubism and Futurism. Born into a wealthy Polish family, she travelled around Europe before ending up in Paris in 1917. Her painting style was bold and colourful and is sometimes described as 'soft Cubism' or 'synthetic Cubism', but it displays Art Deco's cool and sensual nature in its clean, elegant technique. She exhibited for the first time in 1925 and would become the most fashionable portrait painter of her age amongst the well-to-do and the aristocracy. In 1927, she won her first major award, first prize at the Exposition Internationale de Beaux Arts in Bordeaux, France for her portrait *Kizette on the Balcony*.

Paul Manship's sculptural work was on public display outside the Chrysler building and complemented its Art Deco credentials

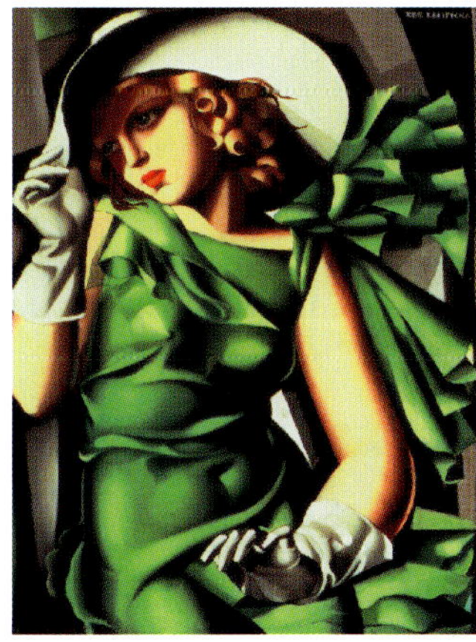

YOUNG GIRL IN GREEN
1927, Oil on canvas, by Tamara de Lempicka, Musée National d'Art Moderne, Centre Pompidou, Paris, France.

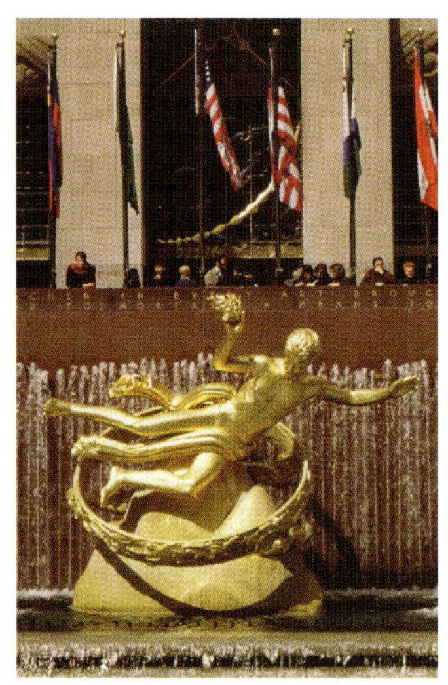

PROMETHEUS FOUNTAIN
Gilded bronze, by Paul Manship, 1934, Rockefeller Centre, Manhattan, New York

He had studied in Rome from 1909 to 1912 and while there became fascinated by archaic art and depicted classical subjects. He also became interested in Indian art and Egyptian, Assyrian and pre-classical Greek sculpture, elements of all of which can be seen in his work. When he returned to America, he found that this mélange of artistic styles was attractive to both sides of the artistic coin – the modernist as well as the conservative, but his simplification of line represented a break from the traditions of Beaux-Arts classicism. He became a precursor of Art Deco and many of his works are considered classics of the style.

Art Deco was the first fashion trend that can be said to have been truly international and even global. It flowered throughout the world, in Australia, Japan, Latin America and South Africa. Evidence of it could be found throughout the arts, but especially in architecture. However, it was in America that Art Deco found its true home. The new and still young country, was hungry for the modern and to lead the world in areas such as manufacturing, and Art Deco was perfect for it. Until the stock market crash in 1929 and the subsequent Depression, America was at the forefront of the style and even afterwards, awaiting the recovery, the movement continued to flower. Extraordinary World's Fairs in Chicago in 1933 and especially in New York in 1939, were celebrations of Art Deco. In 1939 it seemed even to have spread into the world of road-building with plans for streamlined new highways to carry the streamlined new cars and buses that would be made. The credo of the 1939 fair was to show visitors 'the world of tomorrow'. Exhibits included a streamlined pencil sharpener and the main visual feature was the Trylon and Perisphere, a tower 213 m (700 ft) tall, beside which sat a huge sphere, 55 m (180 ft) in diameter. These two futuristic geometric structures in an Art Deco style became the symbols of the fair and featured on publicity material. Six years earlier in Chicago, the 1933 fair boasted buildings of an Art Deco style and the Union Pacific Railroad exhibited its first streamlined train, the M-10000 and the Chicago, Burlington and Quincy Railroad showed off its famous, record-breaking Zephyr. These two trains augured an era of industrial streamlining.

As the austerity of the Second World War arrived, there was no longer any room for good design and cost and function became the overriding necessities of wartime manufacture. Even Clarice Cliff had to stop designing as wartime regulations stipulated that only white crockery was to be produced. Art Deco's star had already begun to fade, anyway, as mass production resulted in a surfeit of goods that many thought were gaudy and created a false image of luxury.

For a brief time, however, Art Deco was the style that defined an age, a style that was accessible to all and a style that filled people with optimism about the future. Above all, its artists and craftspeople have left us with a great number of beautiful and exotic examples of their art.

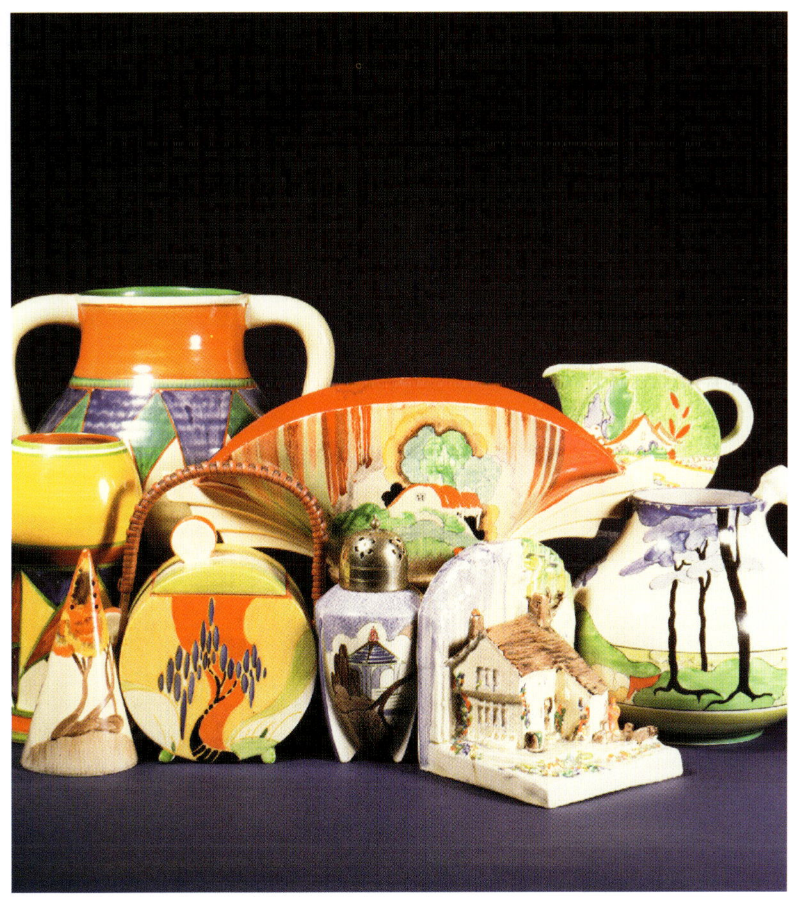

'BIZARRE' SERIES OF CERAMICS
By Clarice Cliff, c. 1928-34. Private collection.

Plate I

VIEW OF THE LIBRARY

View of the library designed by Charles Rennie Mackintosh, c. 1897-99.
Glasgow School of Art, Scotland.

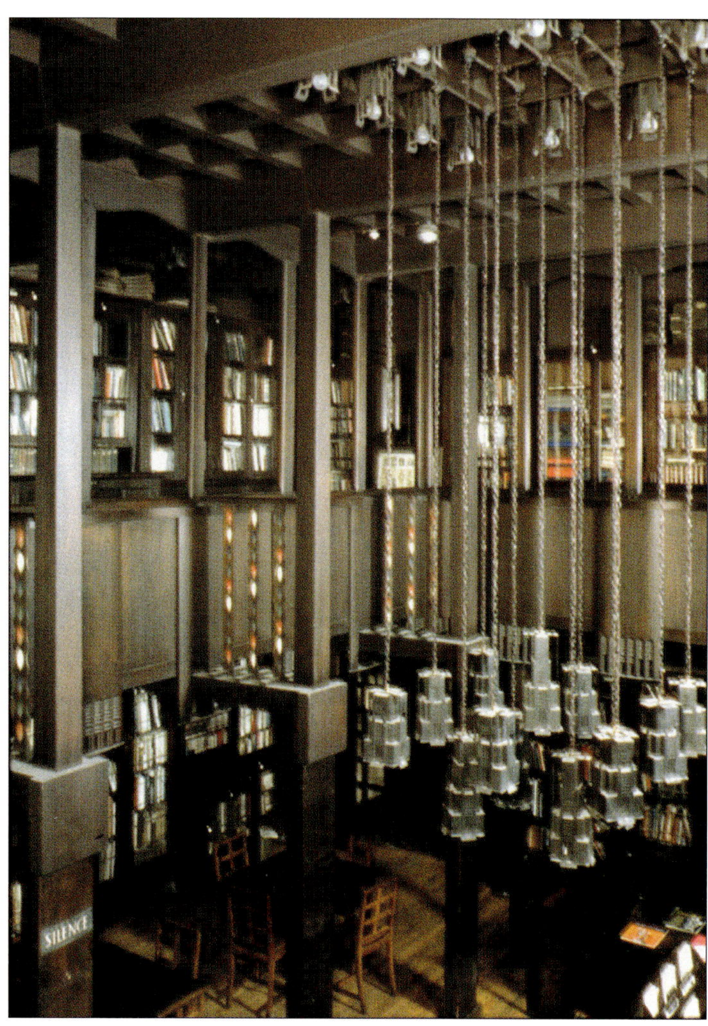

Costume Design

Plate 2

Illustration by Leon Bakst, for a Pas de Deux at the opening gala of the Diaghilev ballet, 1909. Private collection.

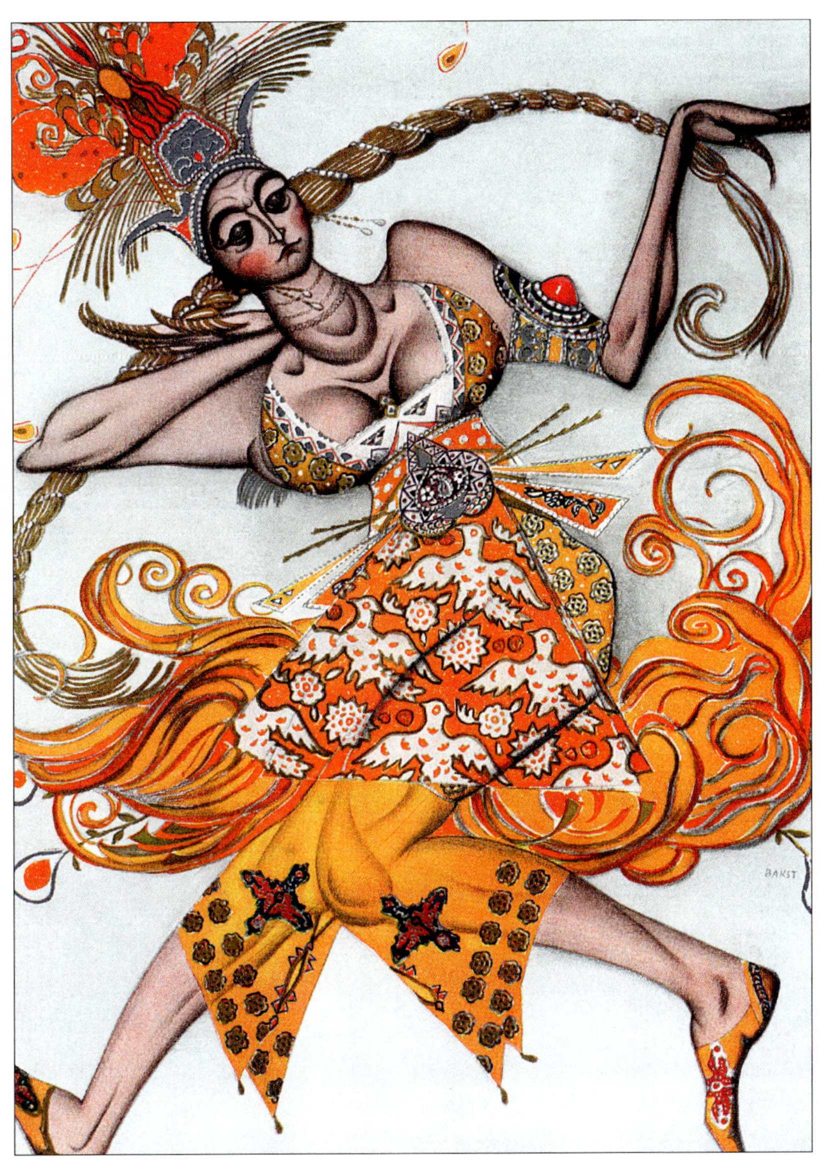

Plate 3

Costume Design

Watercolour on paper, by Leon Bakst, for a Bacchante in 'Narcisse', by Alexander Nickolayevich Tcherepnin, 1911. Private collection.

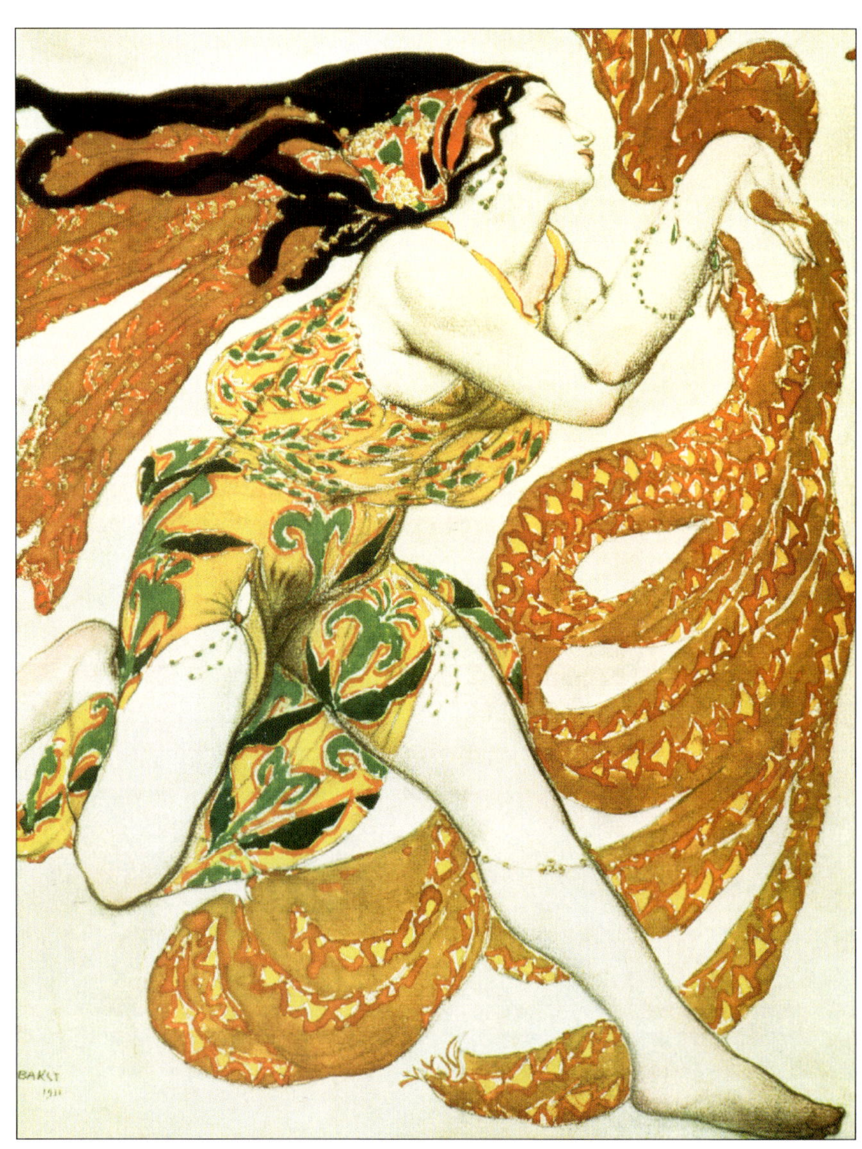

Bibendum Restaurant

Plate 4

Bibendum Restaurant, Michelin Building, SW3, London, designed by Francois Epinasse, c.1911.

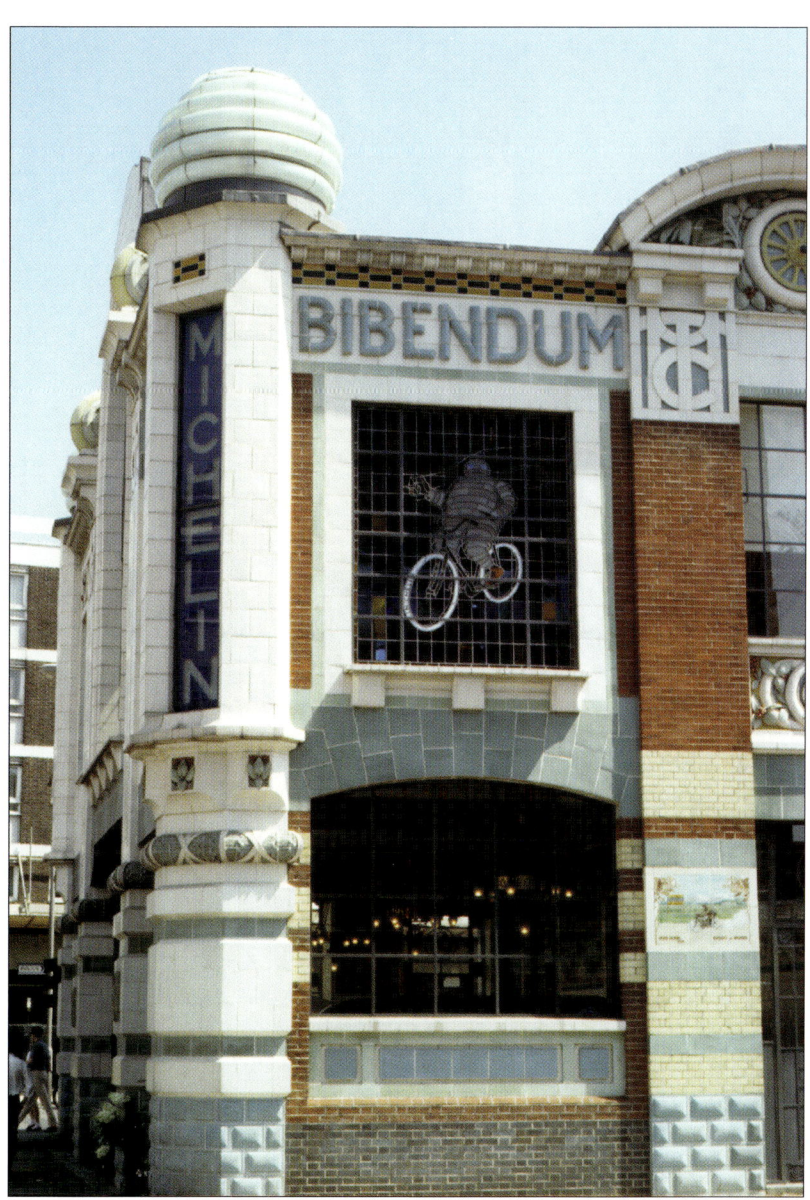

Plate 5

Printing Press

Industrial art design for the 'Journal de la Decoration', edited by Armand Guerinet, colour litho by Willy Pogany, 1911. Private collection.

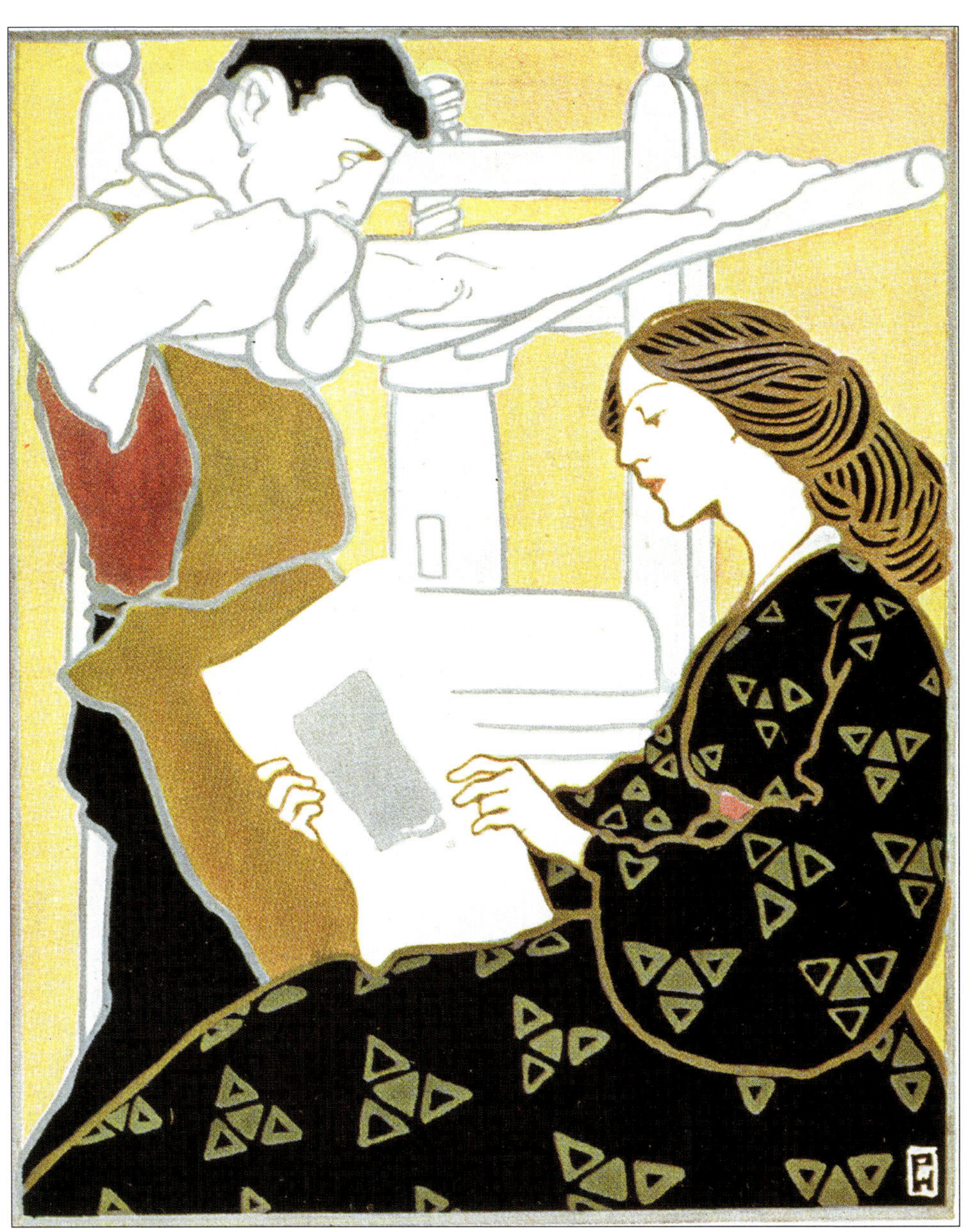

The Wheel

Plate 6

Industrial art design for the 'Journal de la Decoration', edited by Armand Guerinet. Colour litho by Willy Pogany, 1911. Private collection.

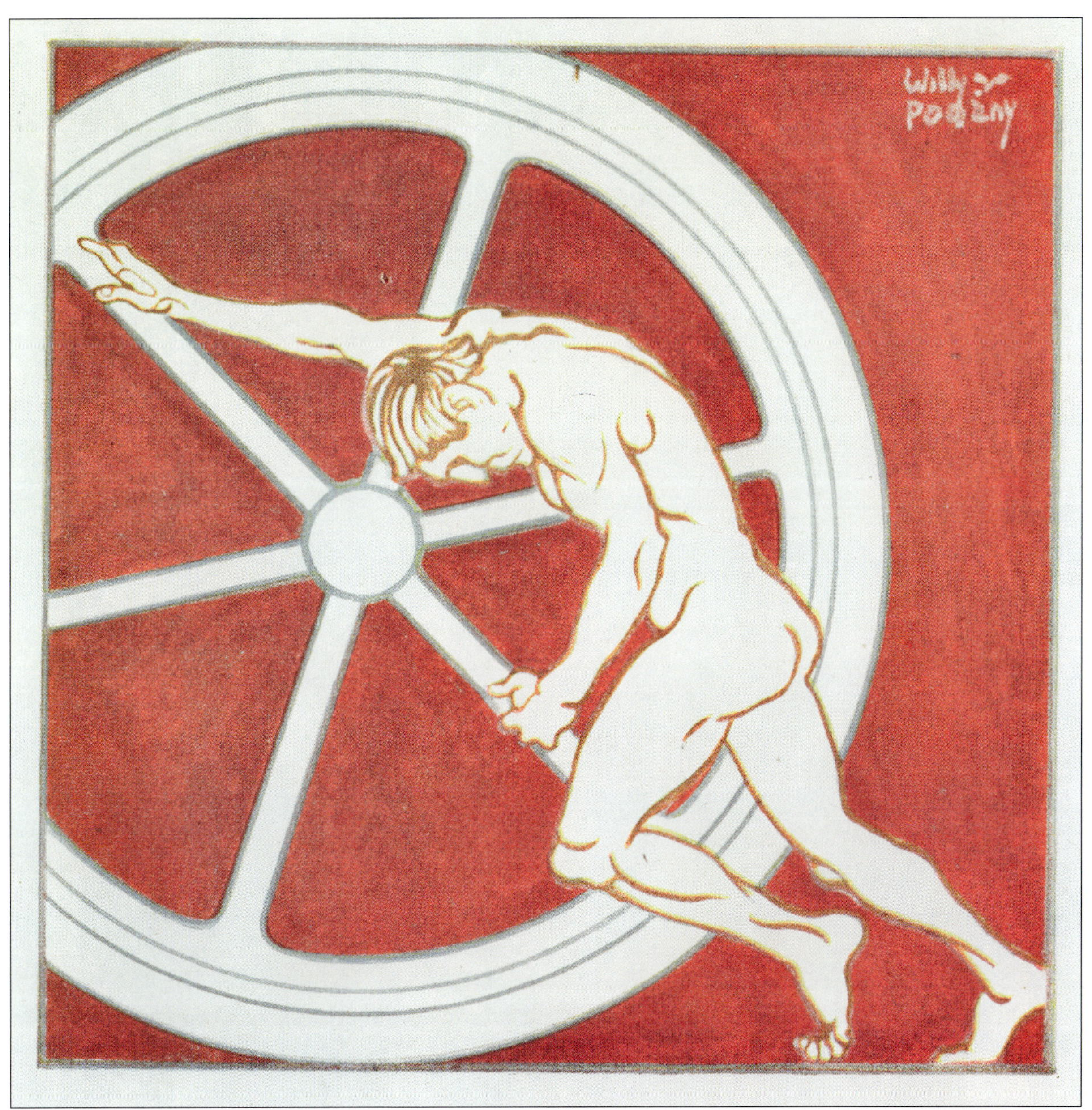

Plate 7

The Turban

from 'Les Choses de Paul Poiret', by Georges Lepape, 1911. Private collection.

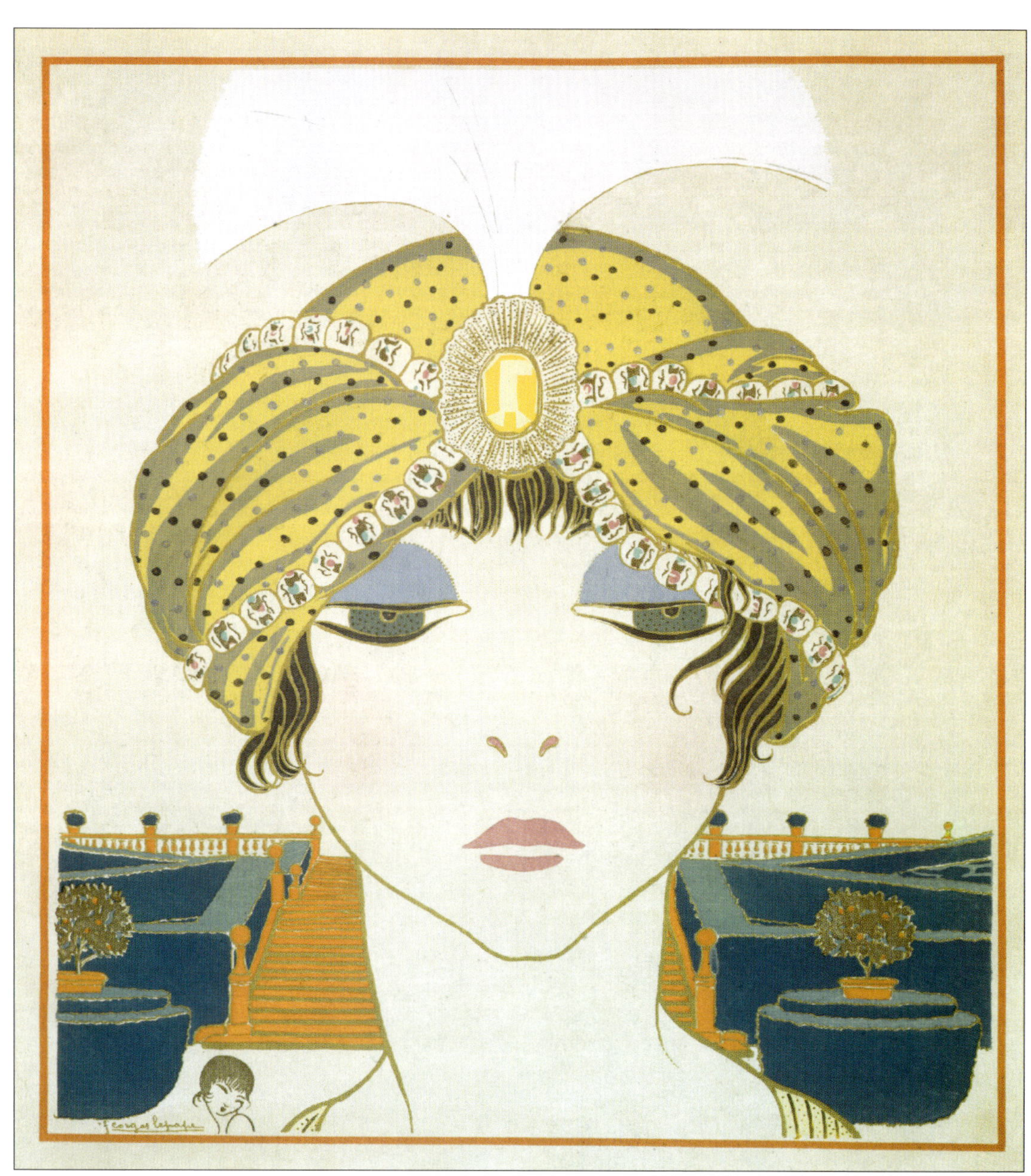

Deutsche Werkbund Austellung

Plate 8

Colour litho, by Peter Behrens, 1914. Victoria and Albert Museum, London, UK.

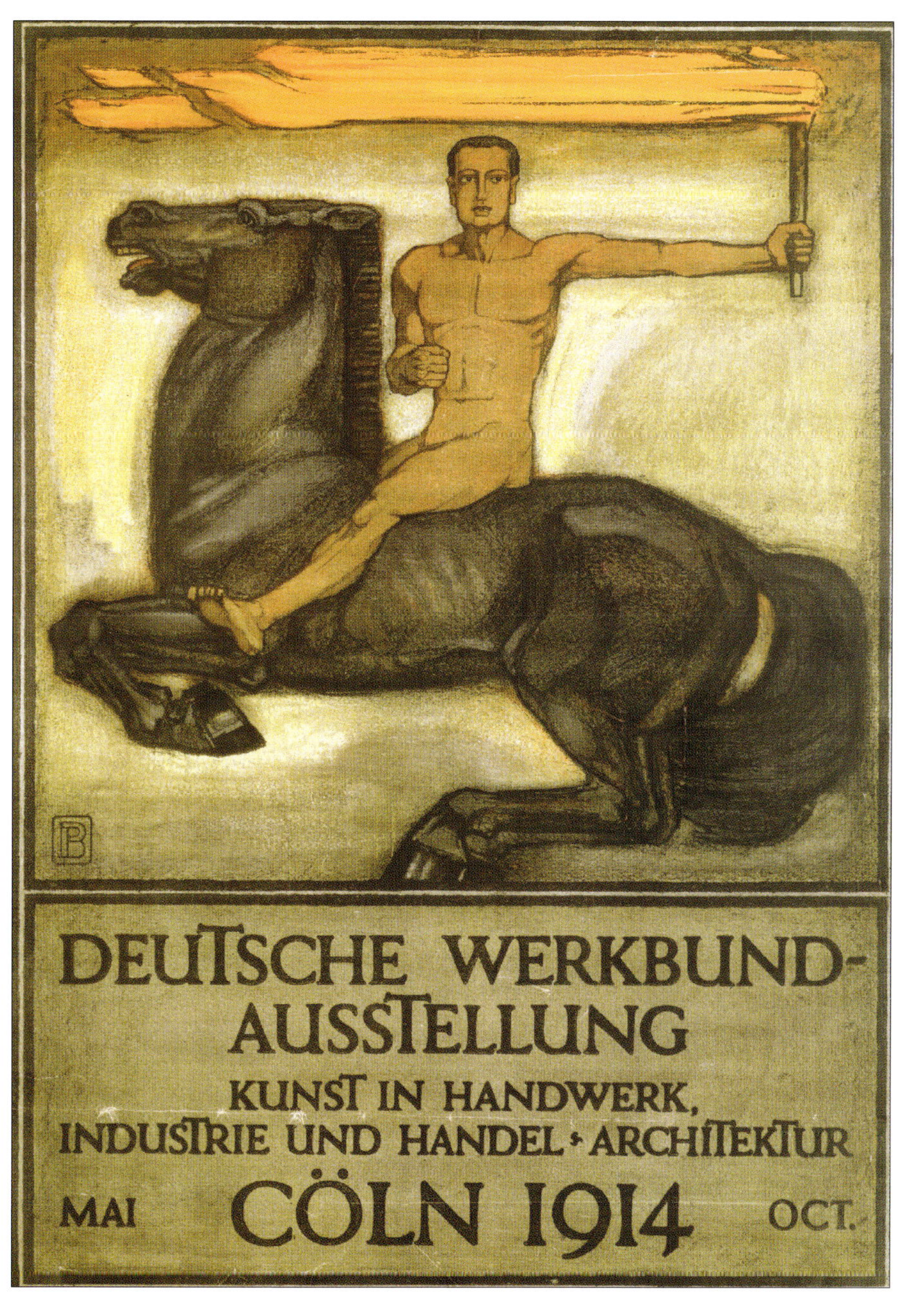

Plate 9

'Die Fledermaus'

Decoration of 'Die Fledermaus', colour litho, artist unknown, German school, c.1915. Private collection.

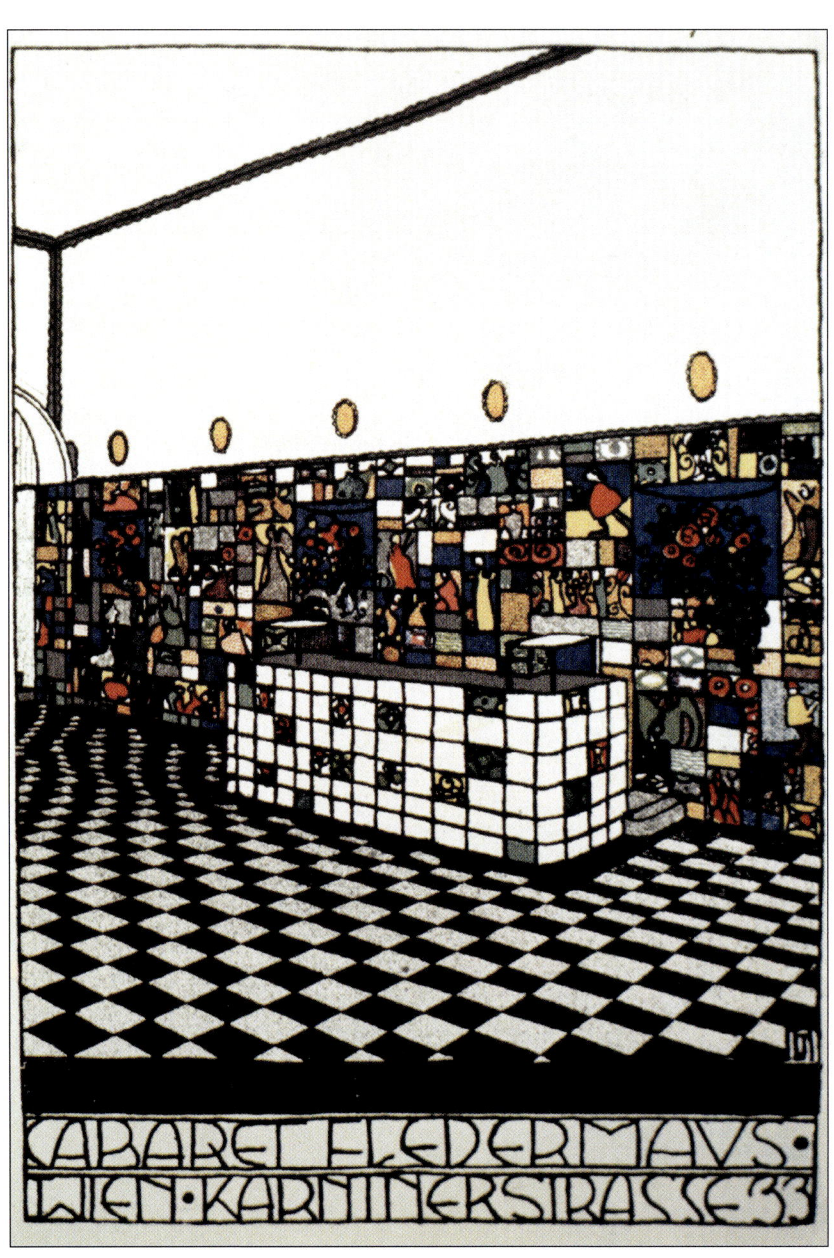

WALLPAPER MEDALLIONS

Plate 10

Scenes from the Ballets Russes, thought to show the dancer Vaslav Nijinsky, artist unknown, c. 1915-1920. Deutsches Tapetenmuseum, Kassel, Germany / © Museumslandschaft Hessen Kassel/ Gabriele Boessert

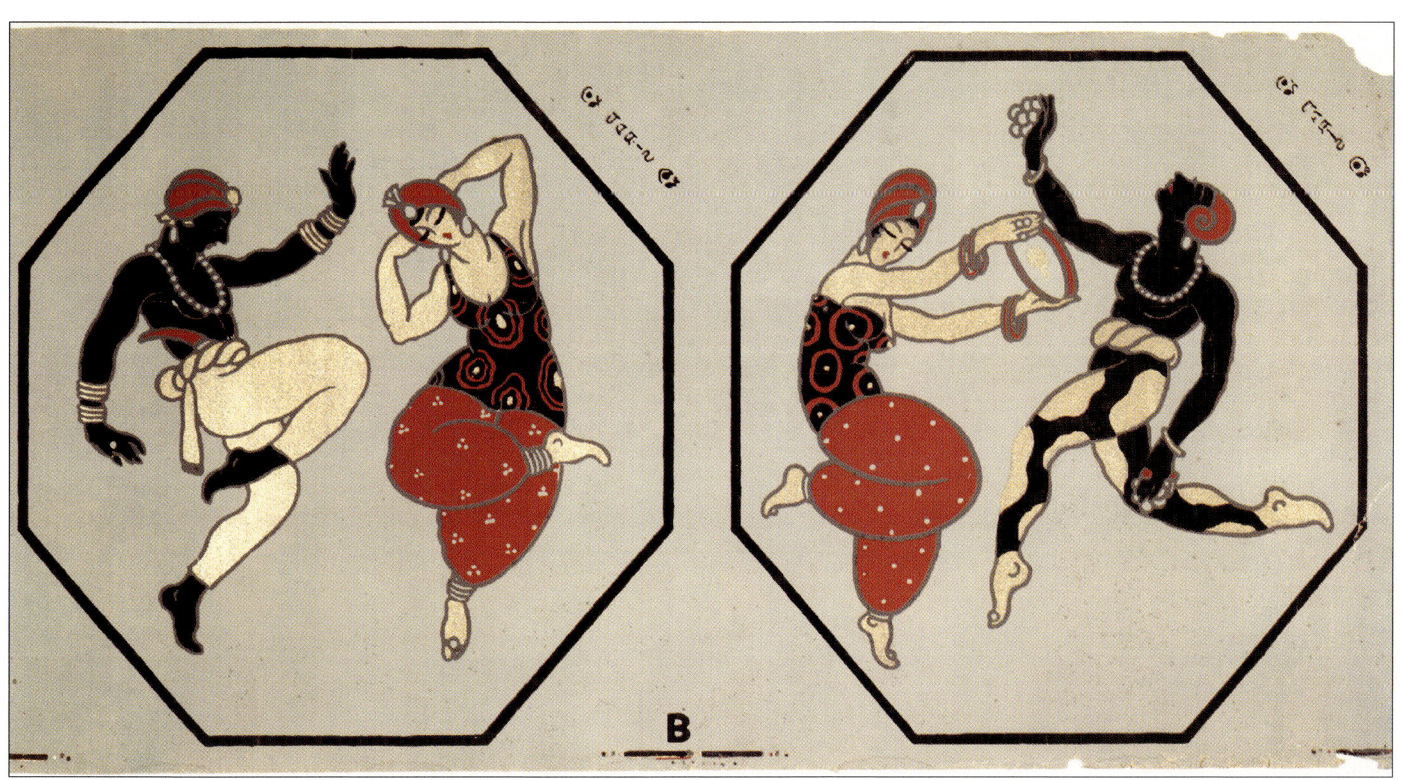

Plate 11

Loading Timber, Southampton Docks

Oil in canvas, by Christopher Richard Wynne Nevinson, 1916-17.

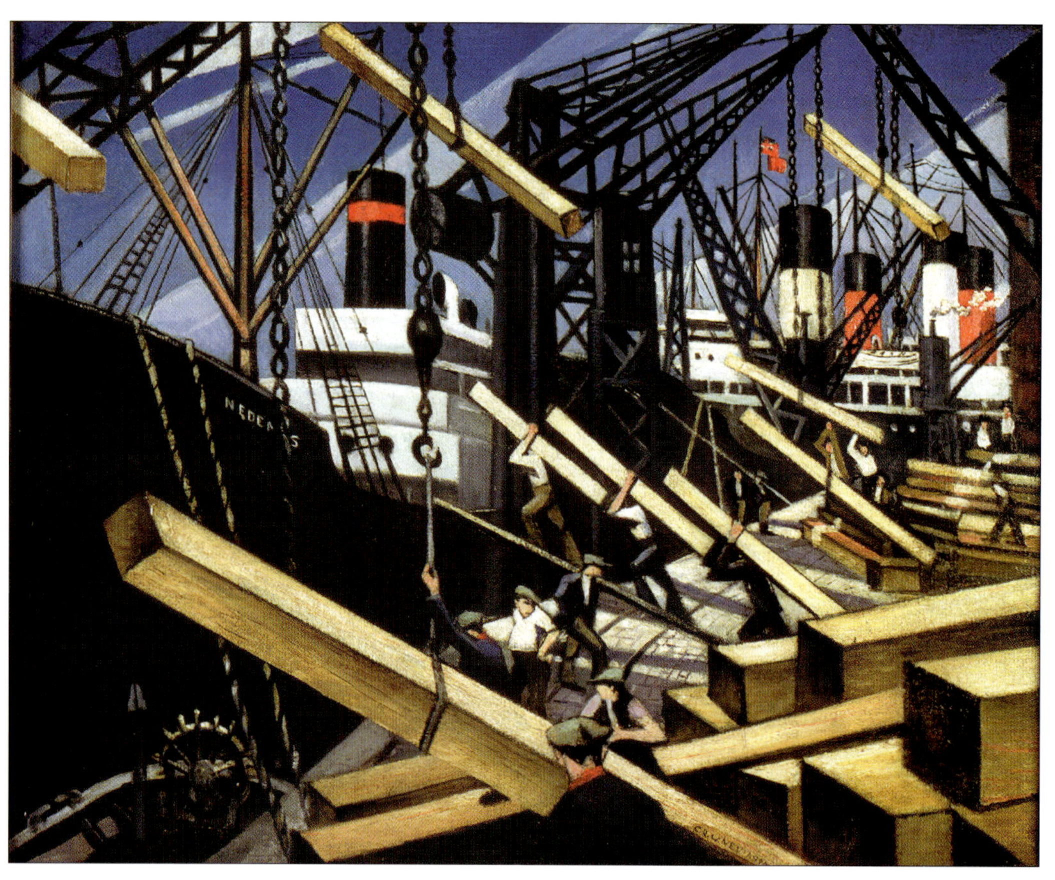

Domino Clock

Ebonized wood with ivory and plastic inlay, by Charles Rennie Mackintosh, 1917.
Art Gallery and Museum, Kelvingrove, Glasgow, Scotland.

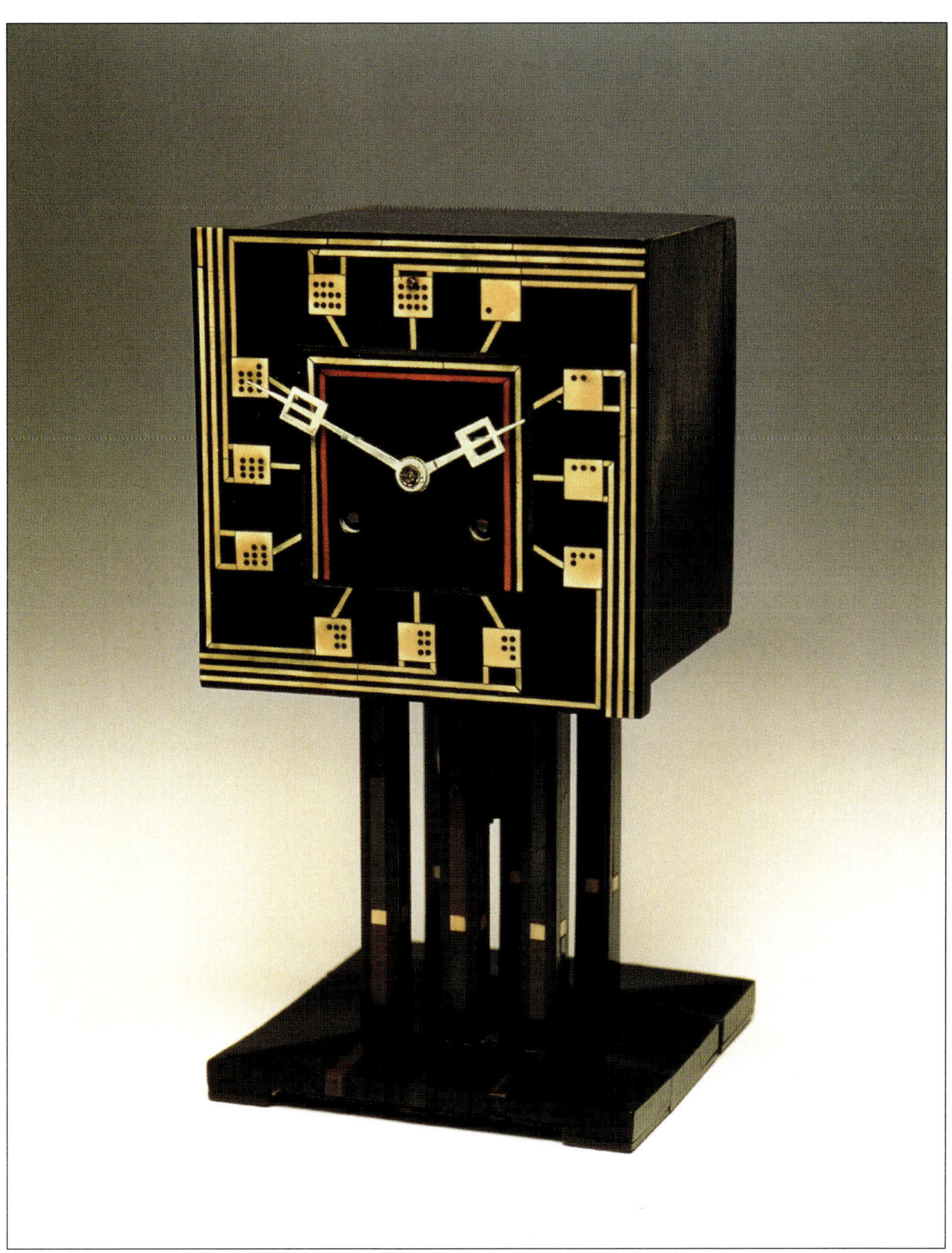

Plate 13

Selection of Art Deco Book Bindings

By various artists, c.1918. Private collection.

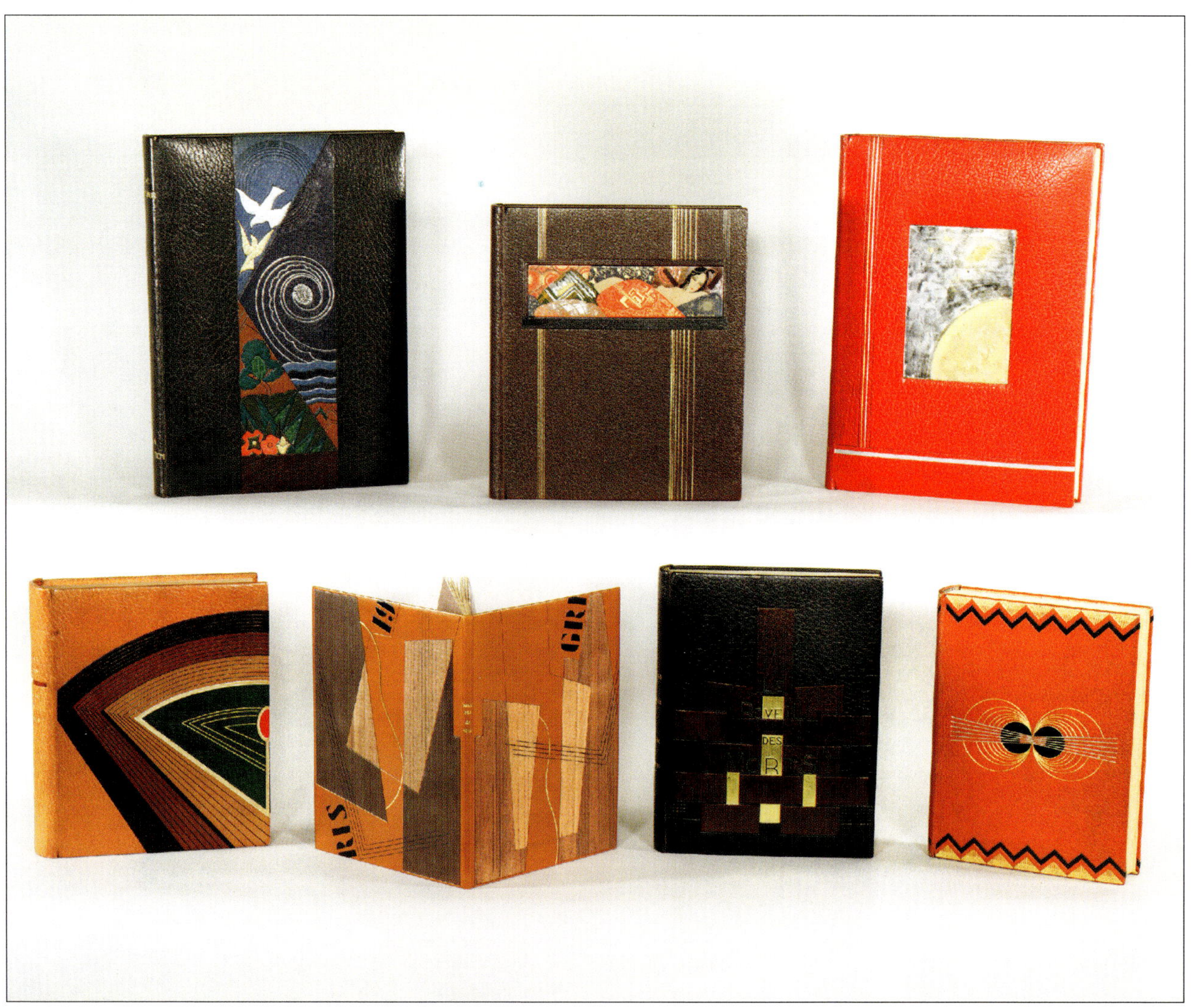

Hercules Upholding the Heavens

Plate 14

Bronze, by Paul Howard Manship, 1918. Museum of Fine Arts, Houston, Texas.

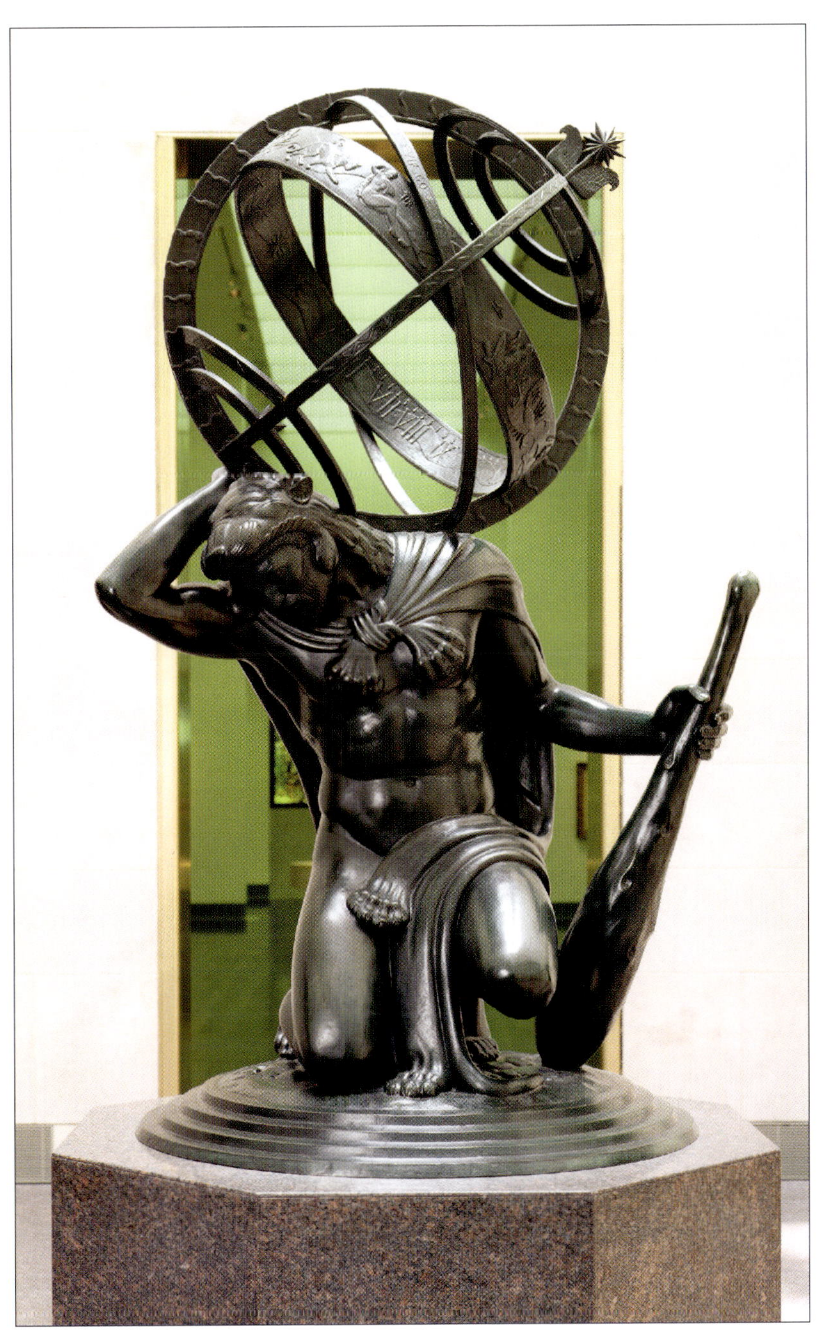

Plate 15

Cinzano Poster

Colour litho by Leonetto Cappiello, 1920. Private collection.

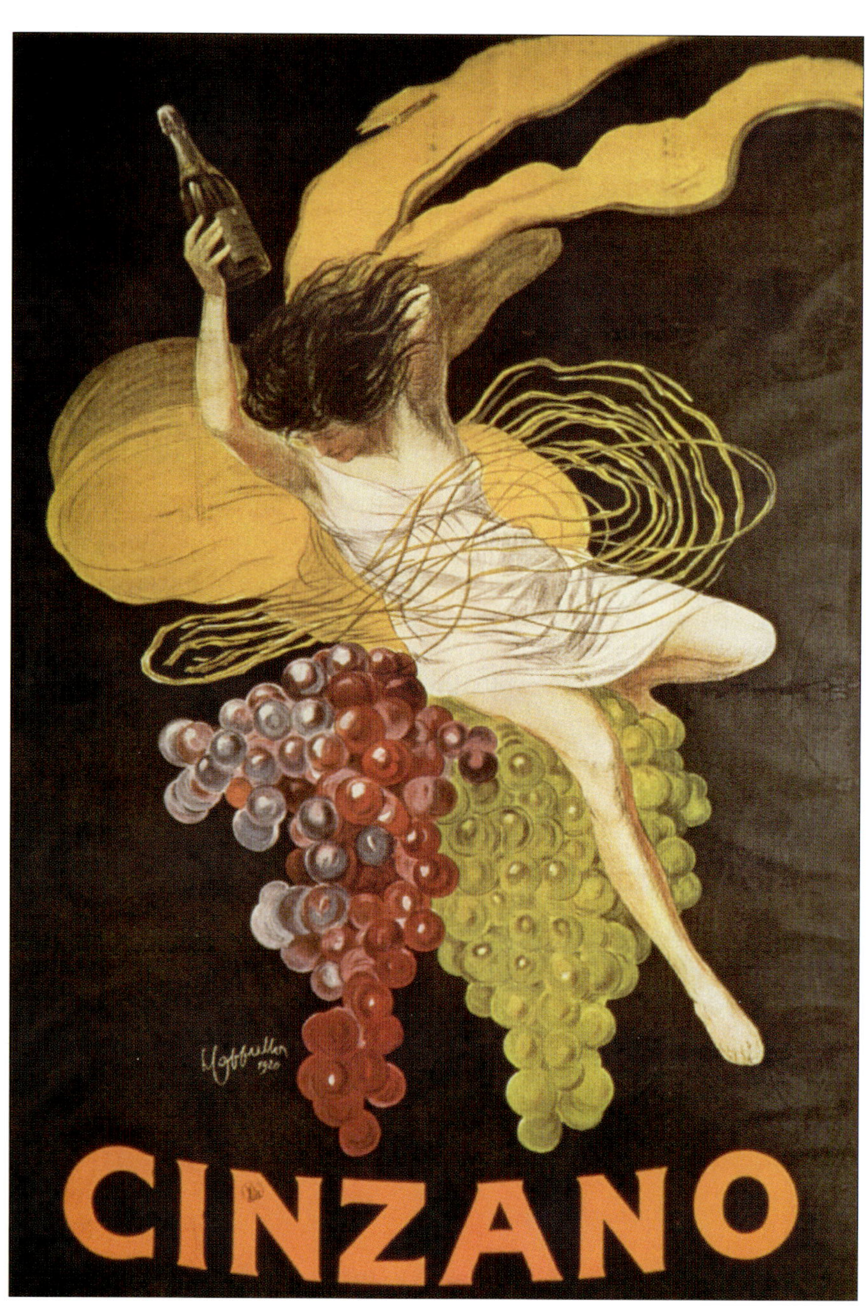

Farewell

Engraving by Henry Reidel, colour litho by Georges Barbier, c. 1920.
Stapleton collection, UK.

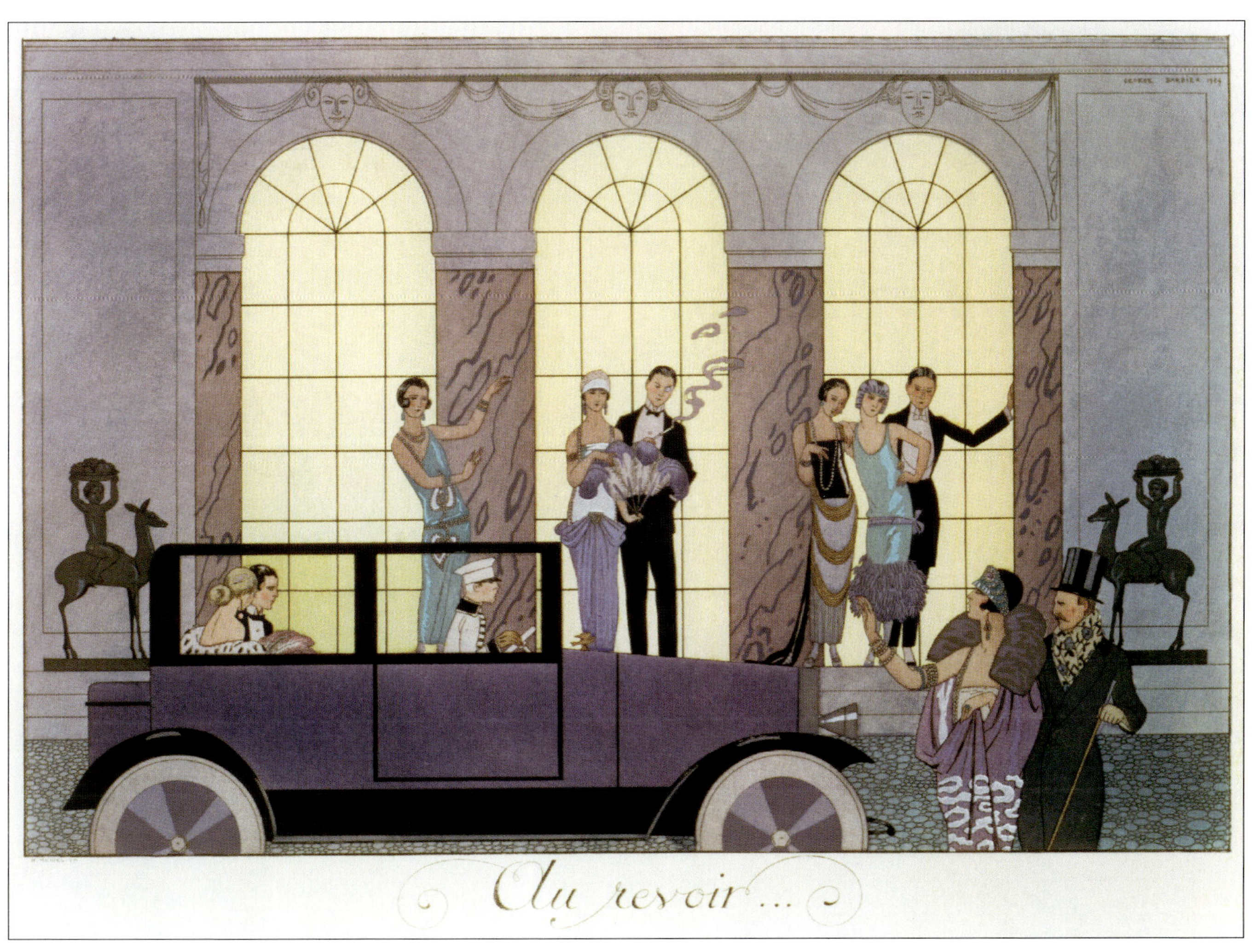

Plate 17

Still Life of Anemones

Watercolour, pencil and gouache, by Charles Rennie Mackintosh, c. 1920
Private collection.

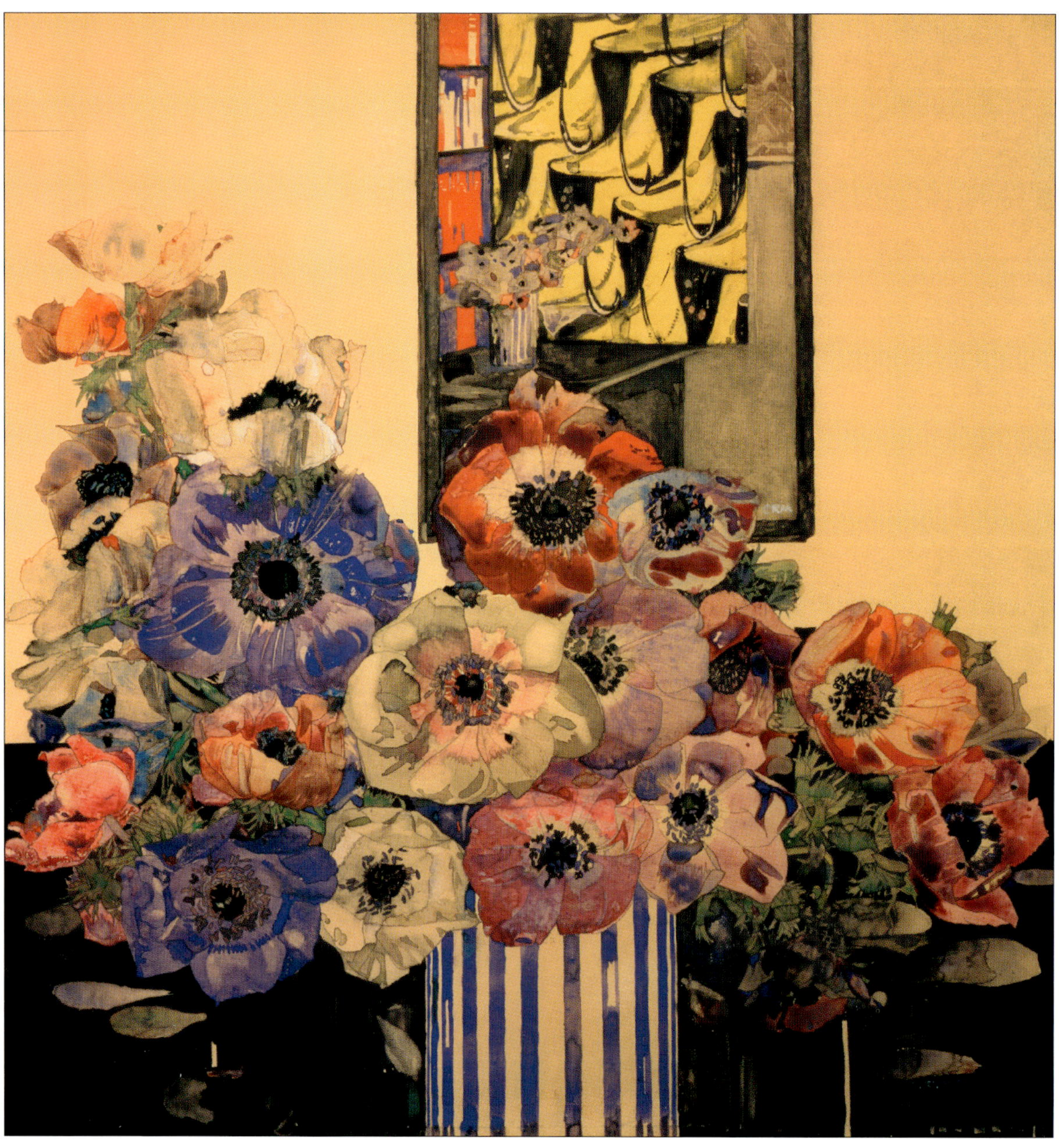

Evening Wedding on the Balcony

Stencil on paper, by Charles Martin, c. 1920. Private collection.

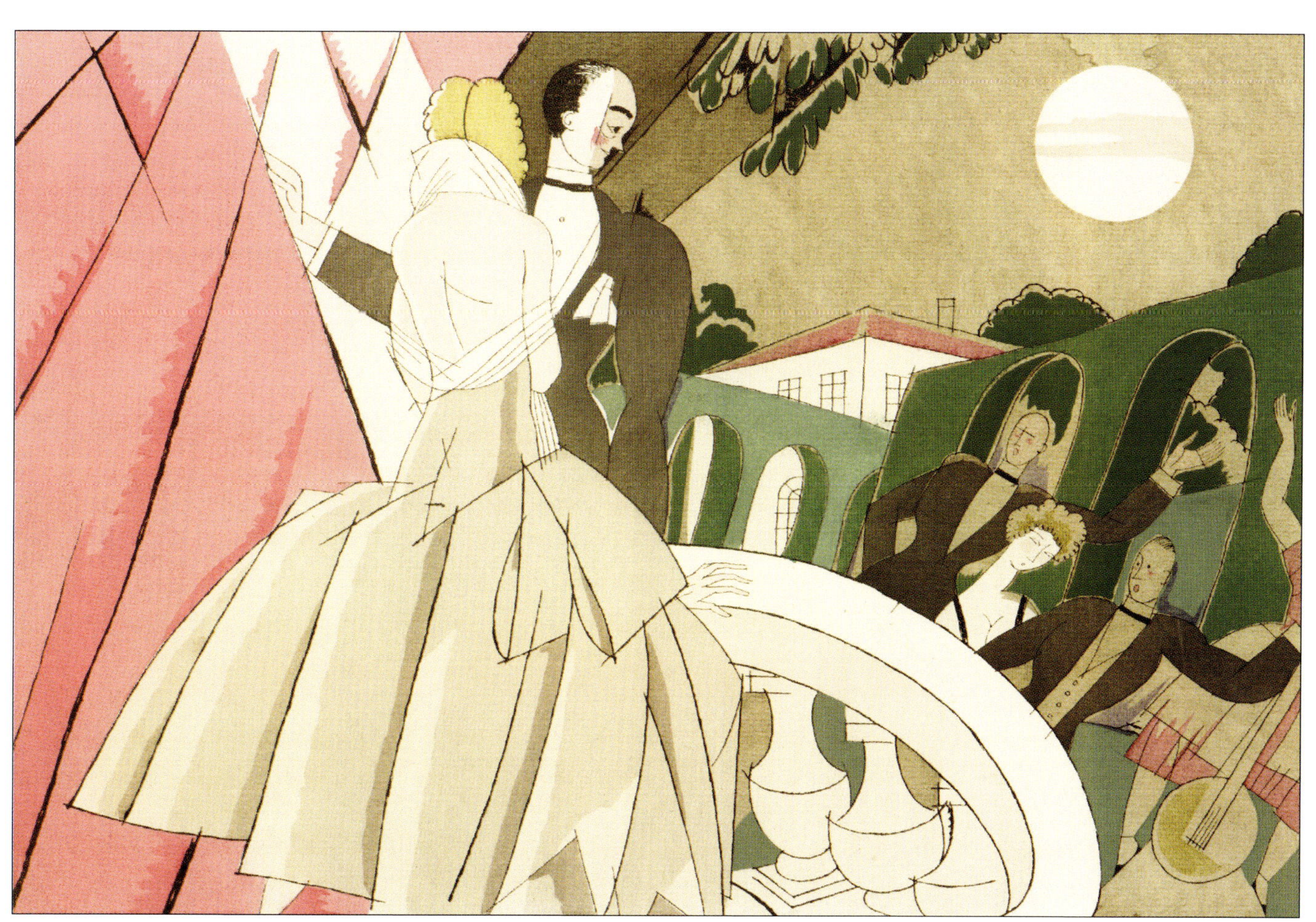

Plate 19

LA TENTATION

Glass and bronze floor lamp, cast as a cobra rising from its basket, by Edgar Brandt and Daum, c 1920s. Private collection.

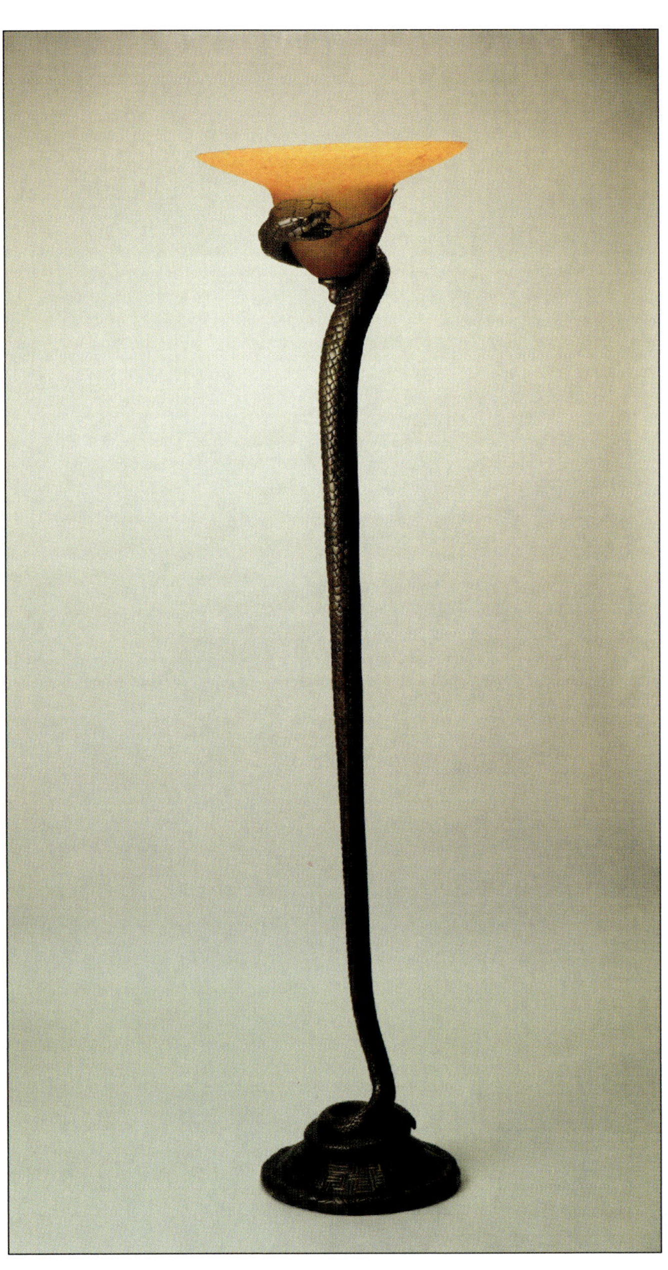

Deux Sirenes Plafonnier

Butterscotch yellow glass, by René Jules Lalique, c. 1921. Private collection.
Photograph © Bonhams, London, UK.

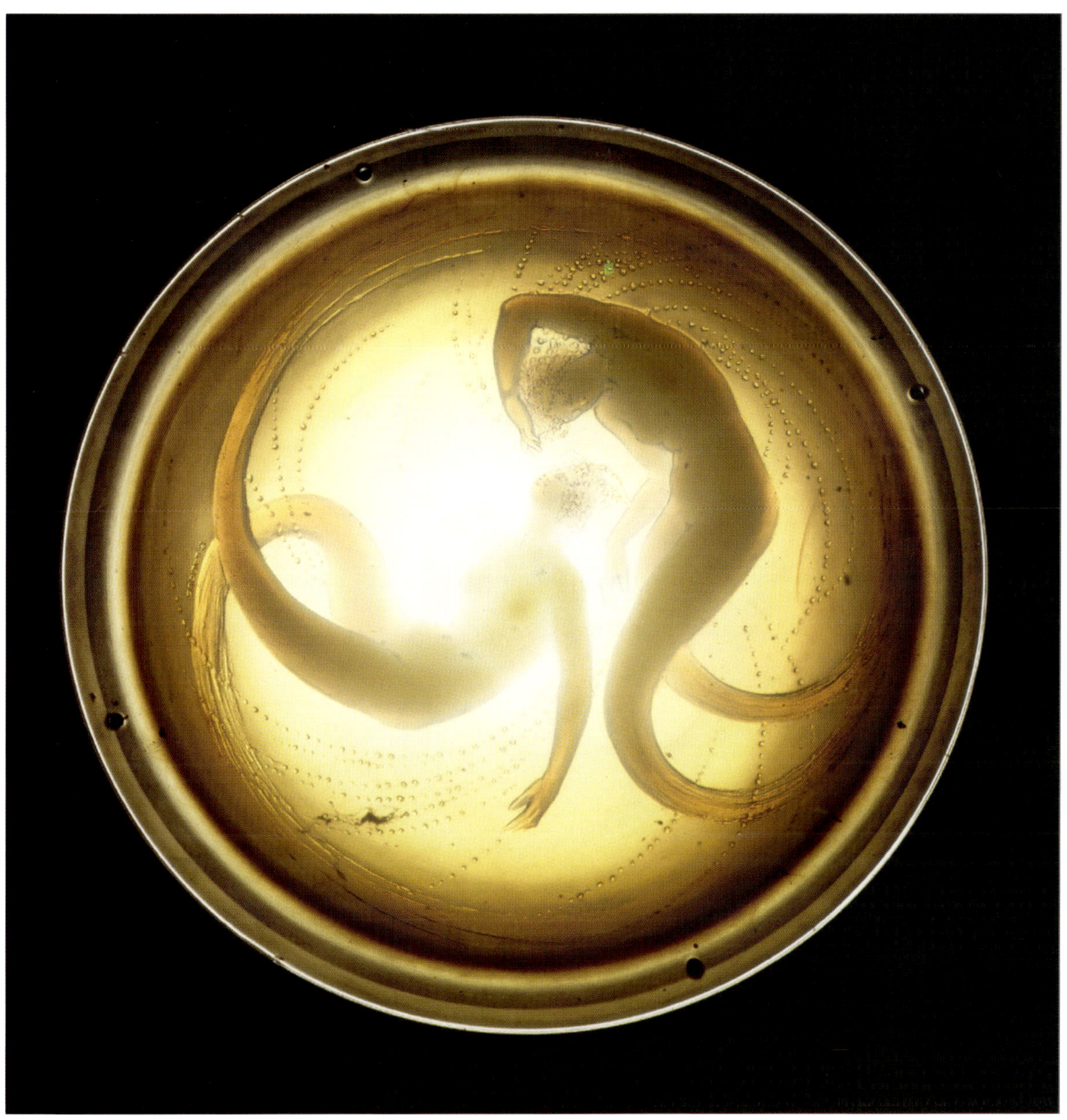

Plate 21

Tennis with Madamoiselle Suzanne Lengien

By René Vincent, 1921. Private collection

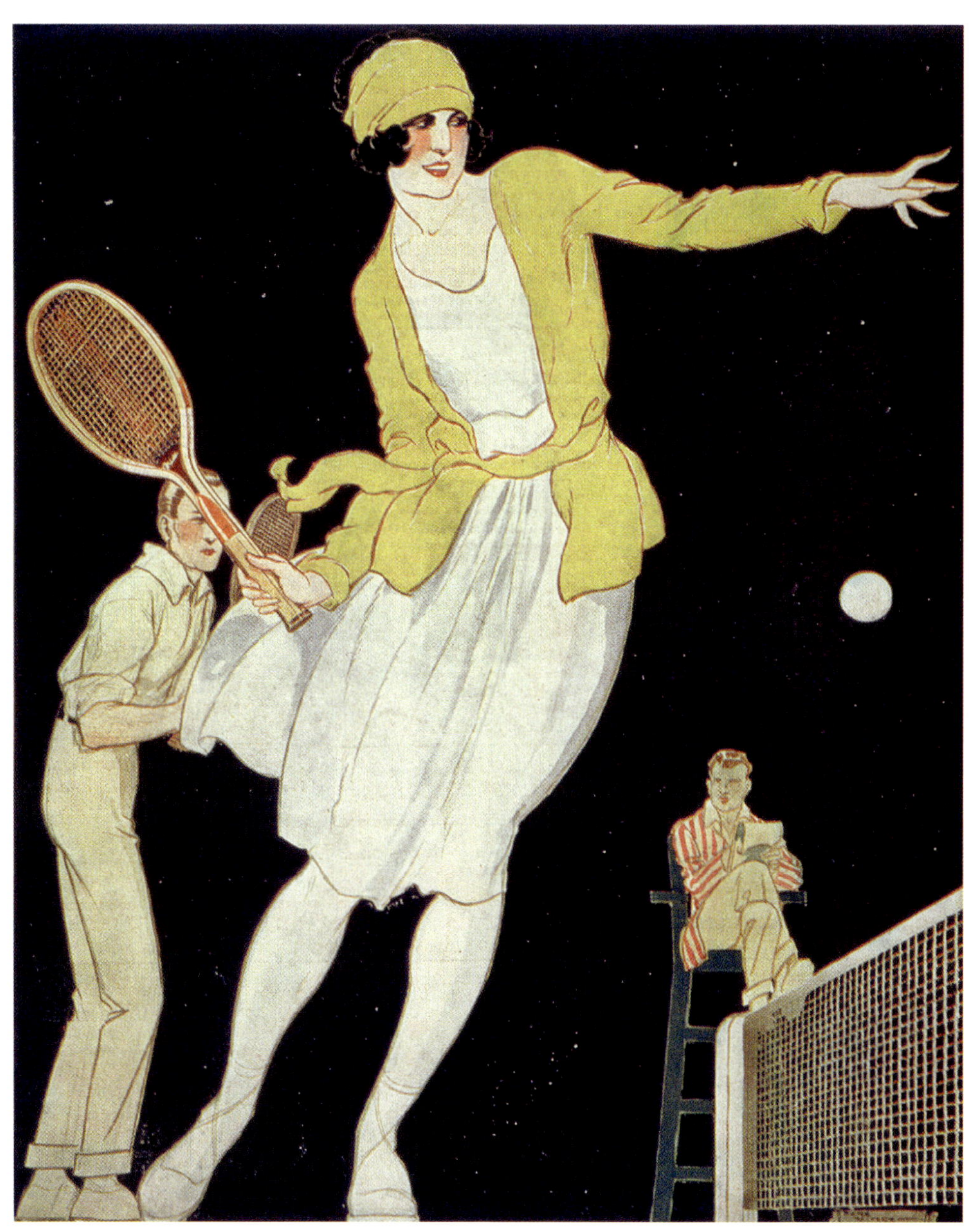

Perspective

Plate 22

Oil on canvas, by Tamara de Lempicka, 1923. Petit Palais, Geneva, Switzerland.

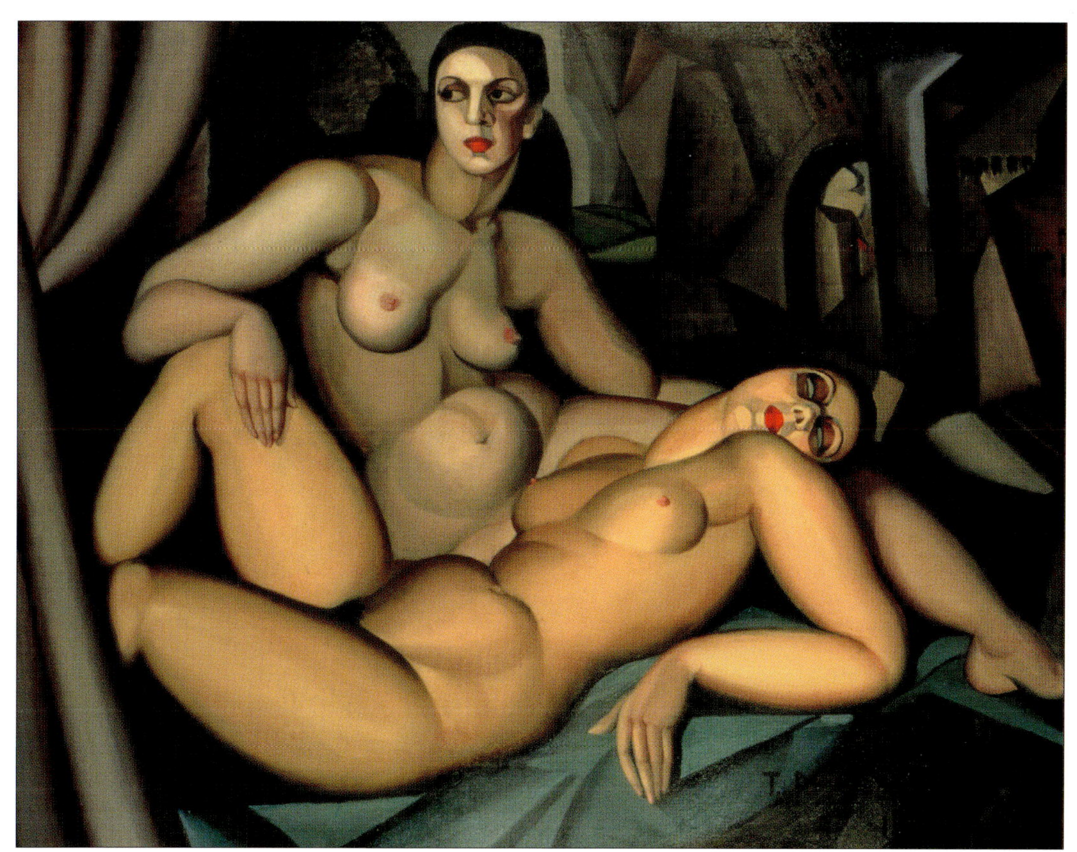

Plate 23 Perruches Electric Blue Vase

Glass vase, by René Jules Lalique, c.1923. Private collection.
Photograph © Bonhams, London, UK.

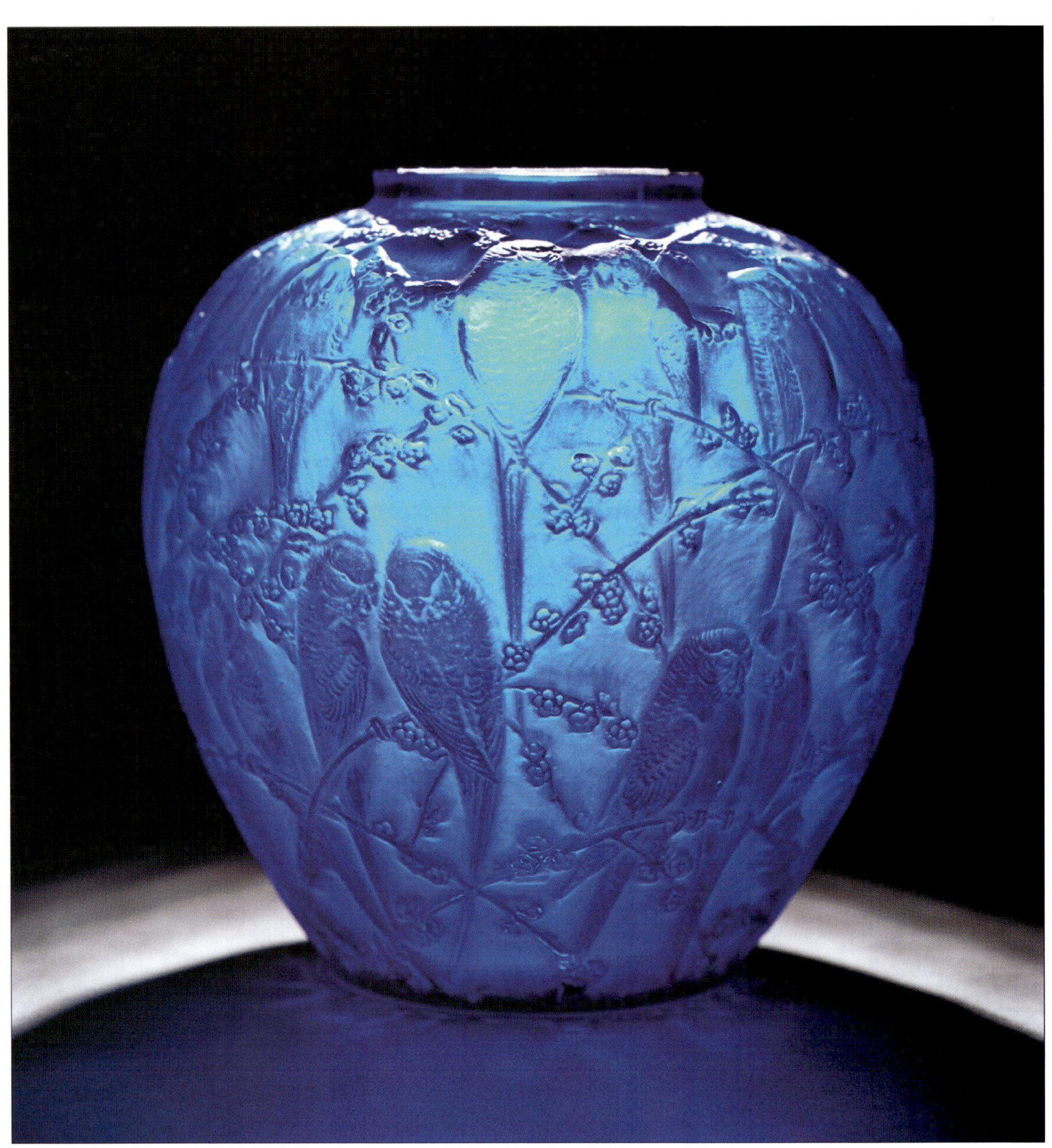

INNOCENCE

Plate 24

Ivory and bronze with a marble base, by Dimitri Chiparus, c. 1925. Private collection.

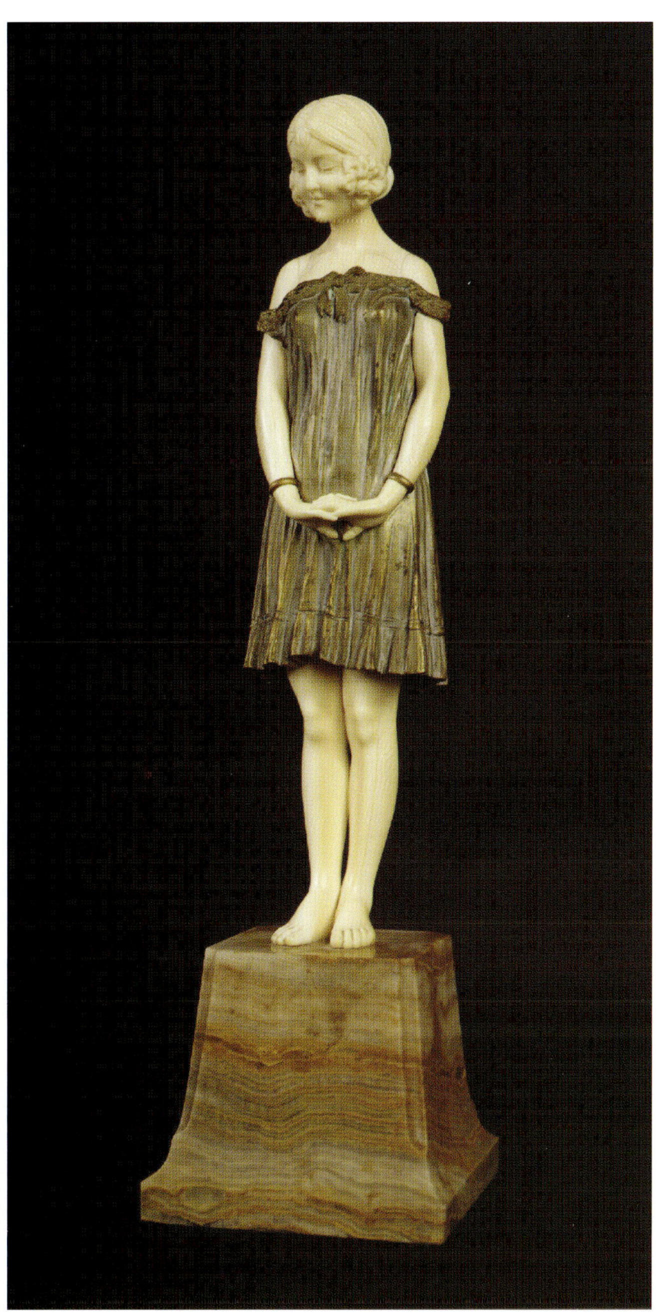

Plate 25

Dancer of Kapurthala

Gold painted gilt bronze and ivory, by Dimitri Chiparus, c. 1925.
Private collection.

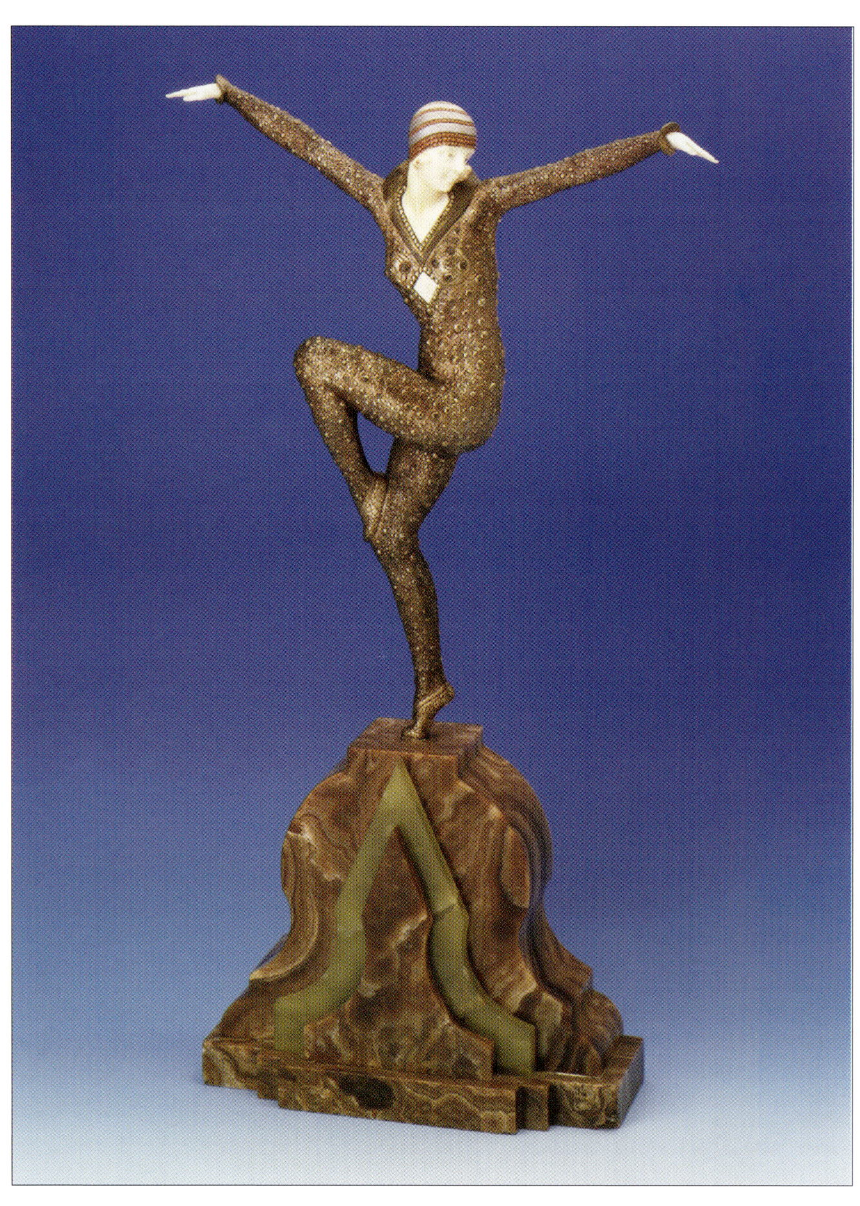

Ayouta

Gold painted gilt bronze and ivory, by Dimitri Chiparus, c 1925.
Private collection.

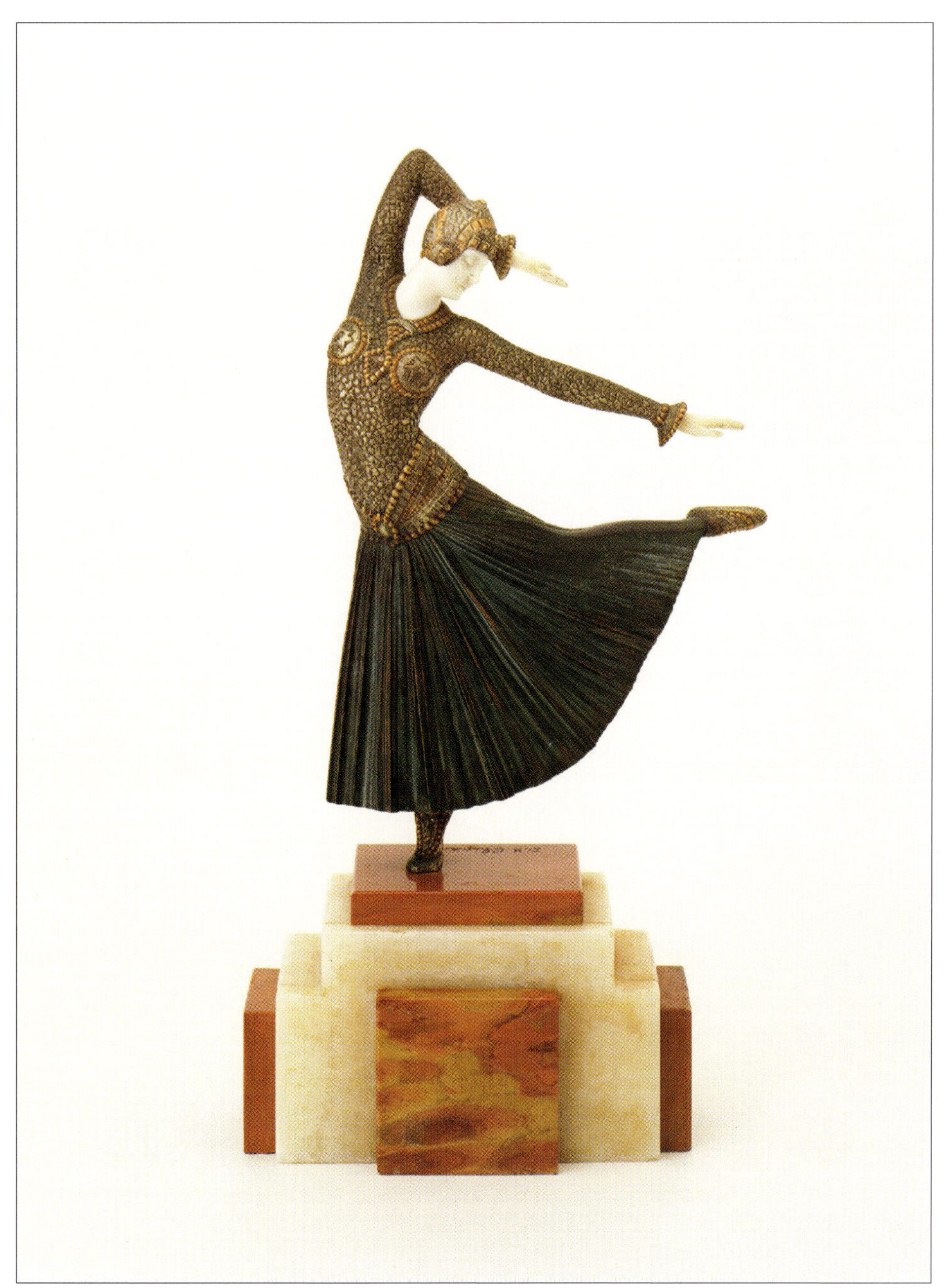

Dining Room

Dining room designed by Maurice Dufrene, from 'Interieurs en Couleurs', 1925.
Private collection

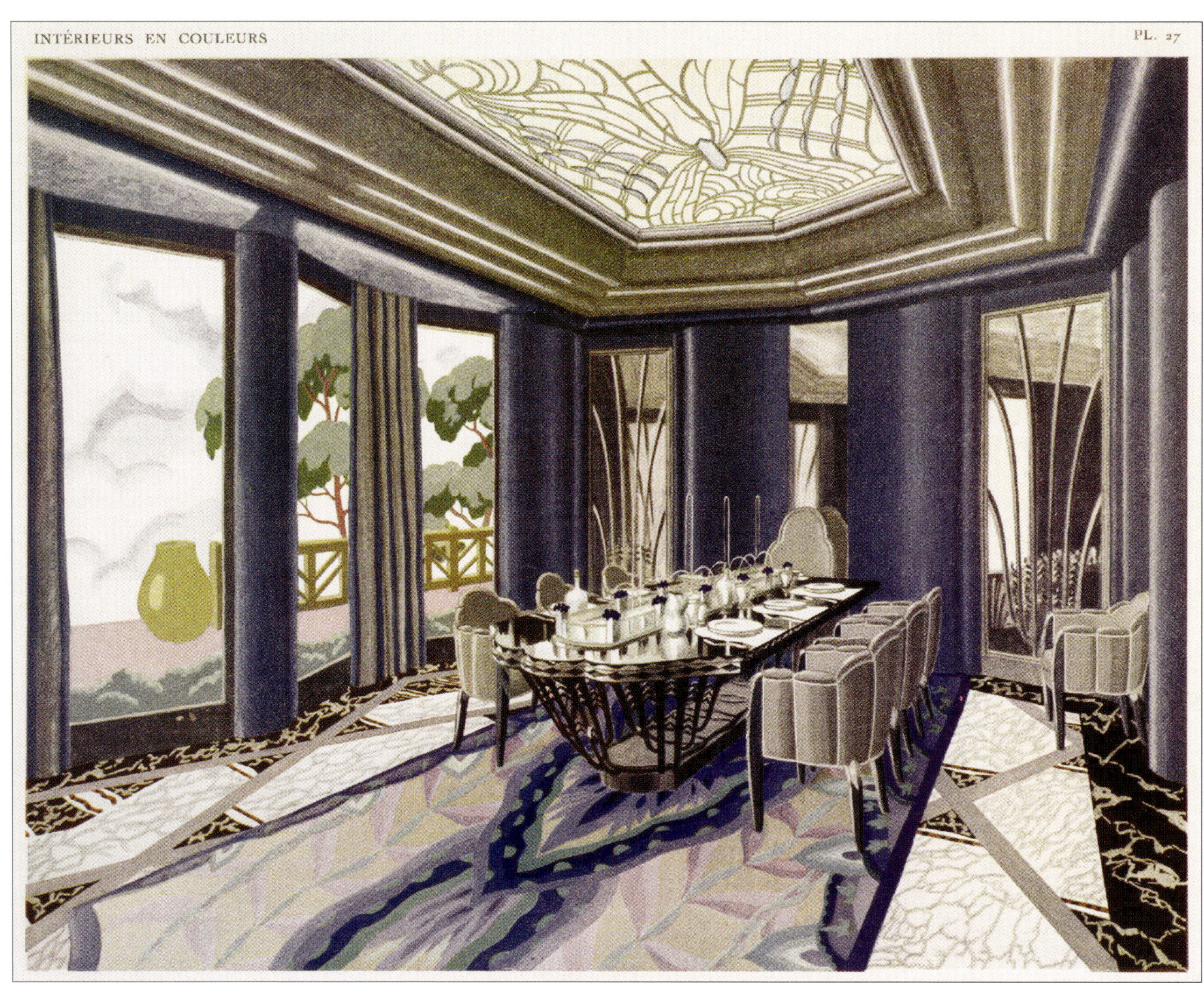

Table with Stool

by Jean Dunand, c. 1925. Private collection.

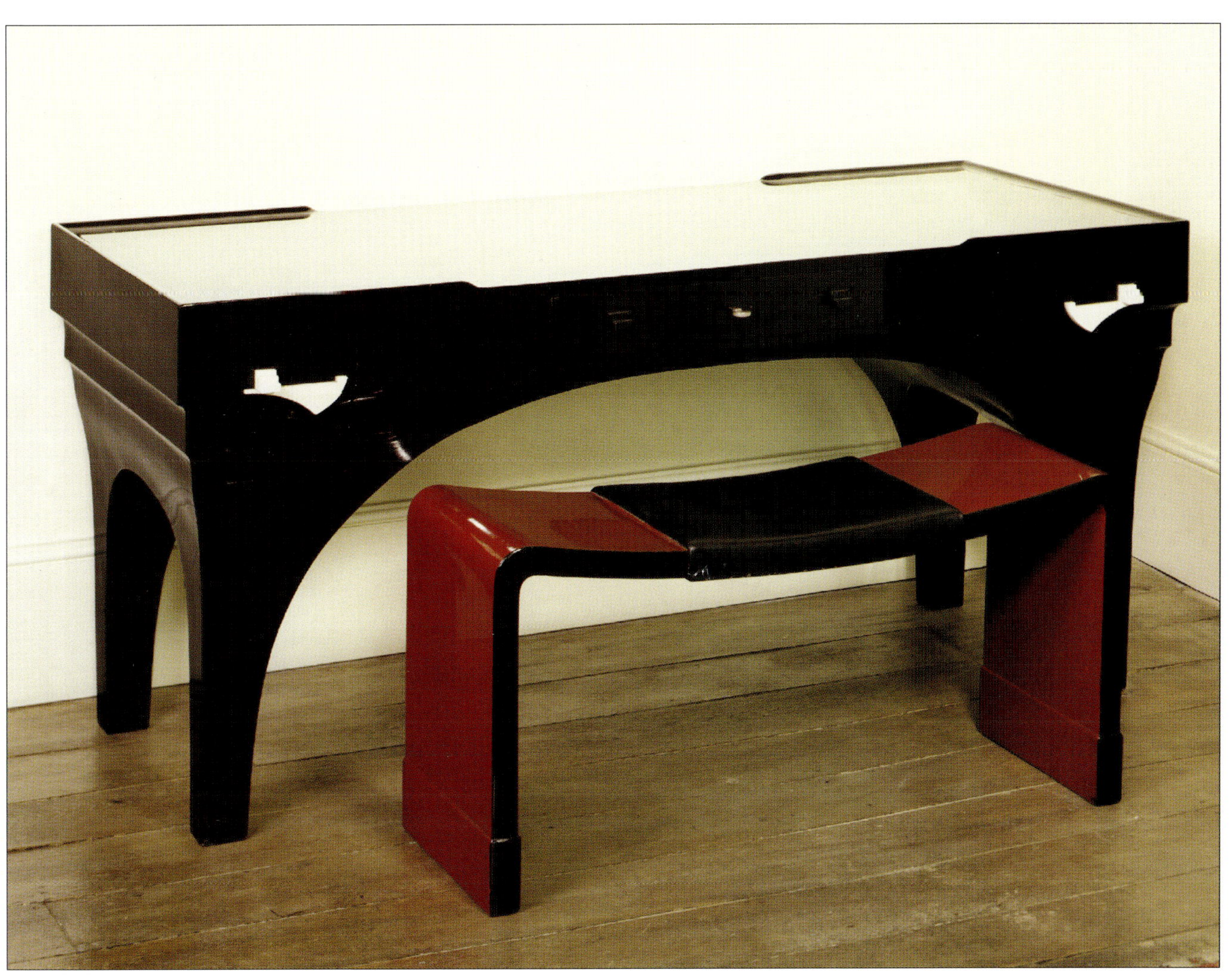

Plate 29

Pendant

Ivory, onyx and coral, inset with diamonds, by Georges Fouquet, c 1925.
Private collection.

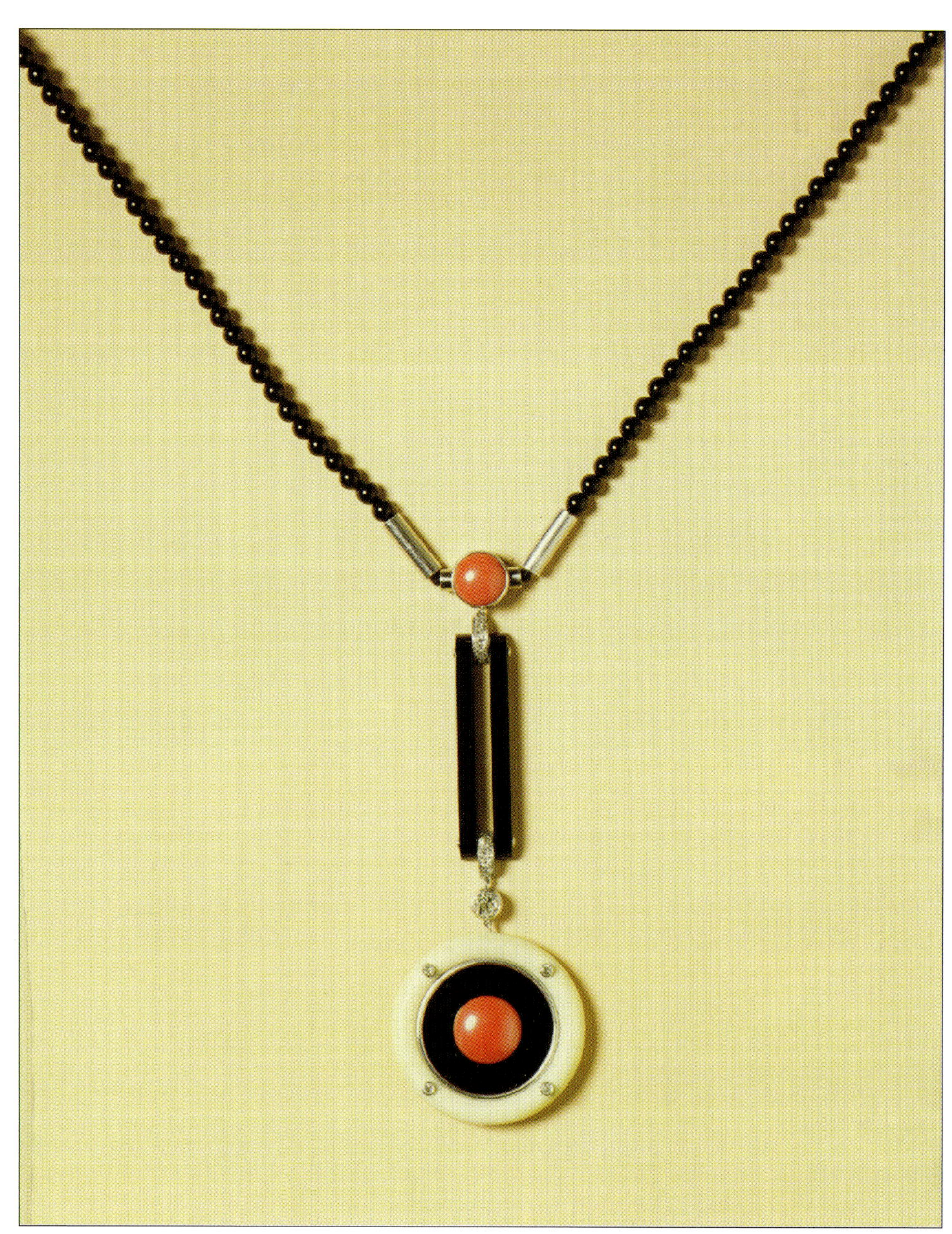

THE FLIGHT OF EUROPA

Gilt bronze on marble base, by Paul Howard Manship, 1925. Indianapolis Museum of Art, USA.

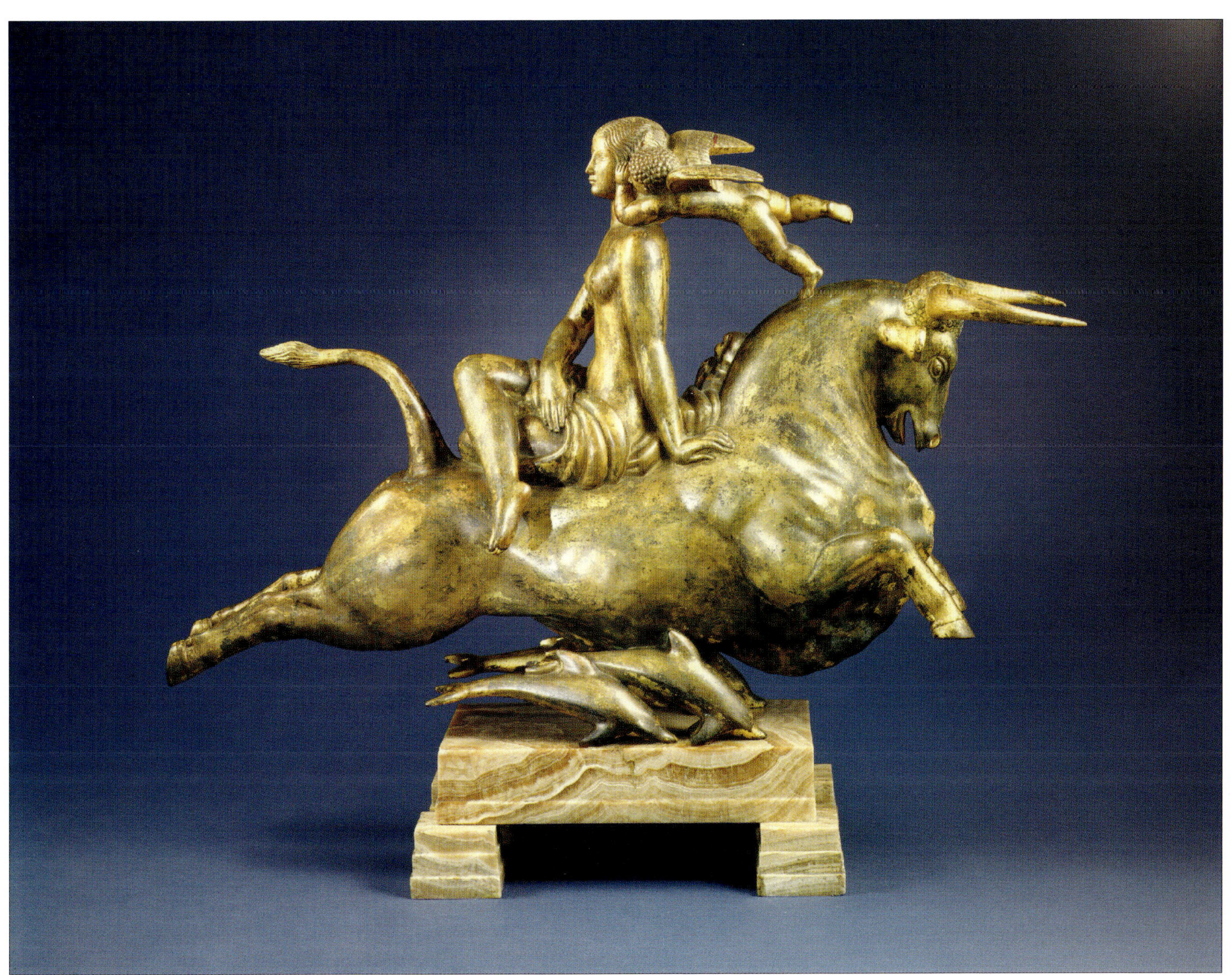

Plate 31

Salon for an Ambassador

A project for the Exposition des Arts Decoratifs.
Colour litho, by Henri Rapin, 1925. Bibliotheque des Arts Decoratifs, Paris, France.

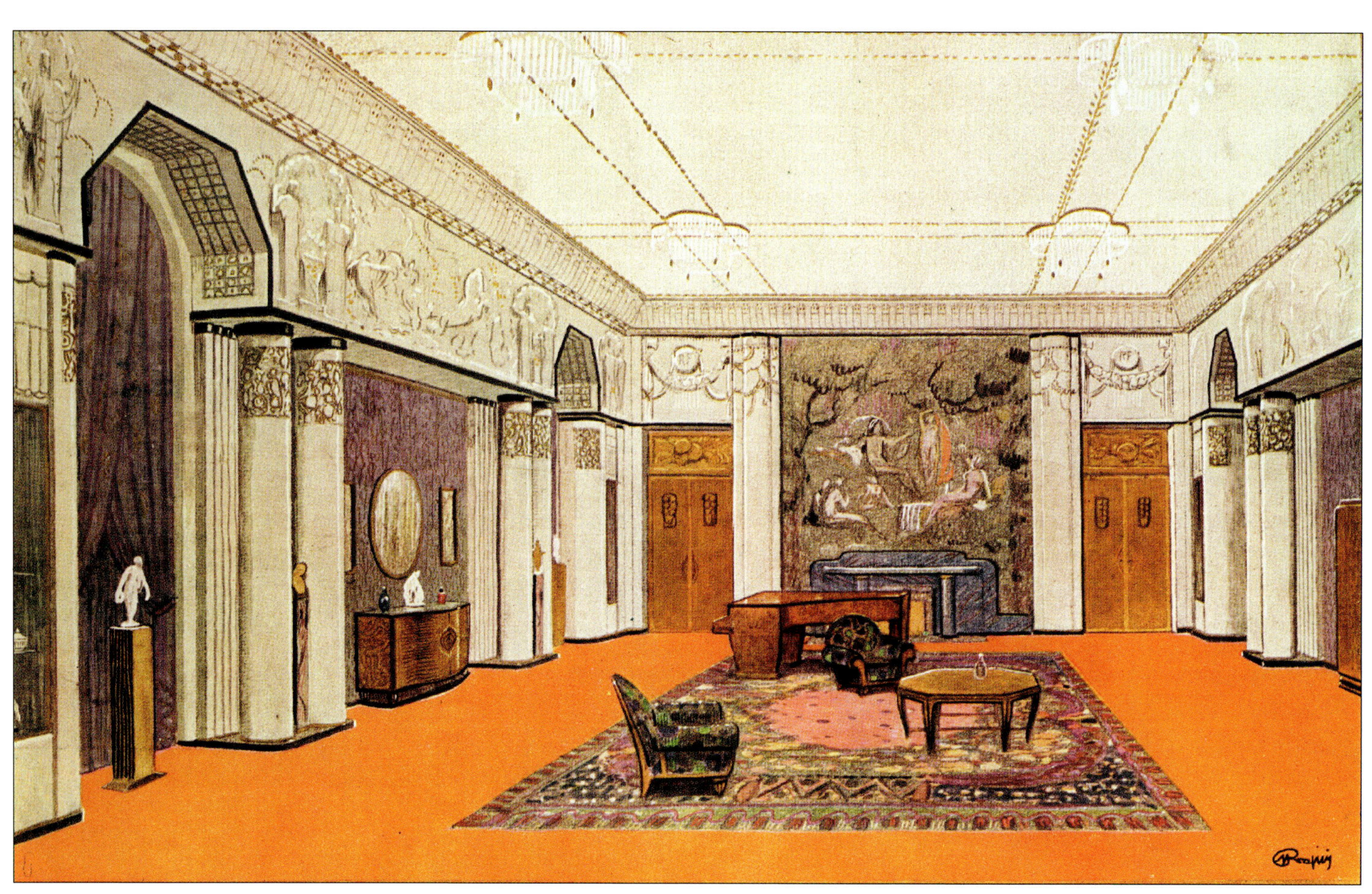

Bedroom

Bedroom for Ensembles Mobiliers II, exposition Interior, Paris, designed by J. Ruhlmann, 1925. Private collection.

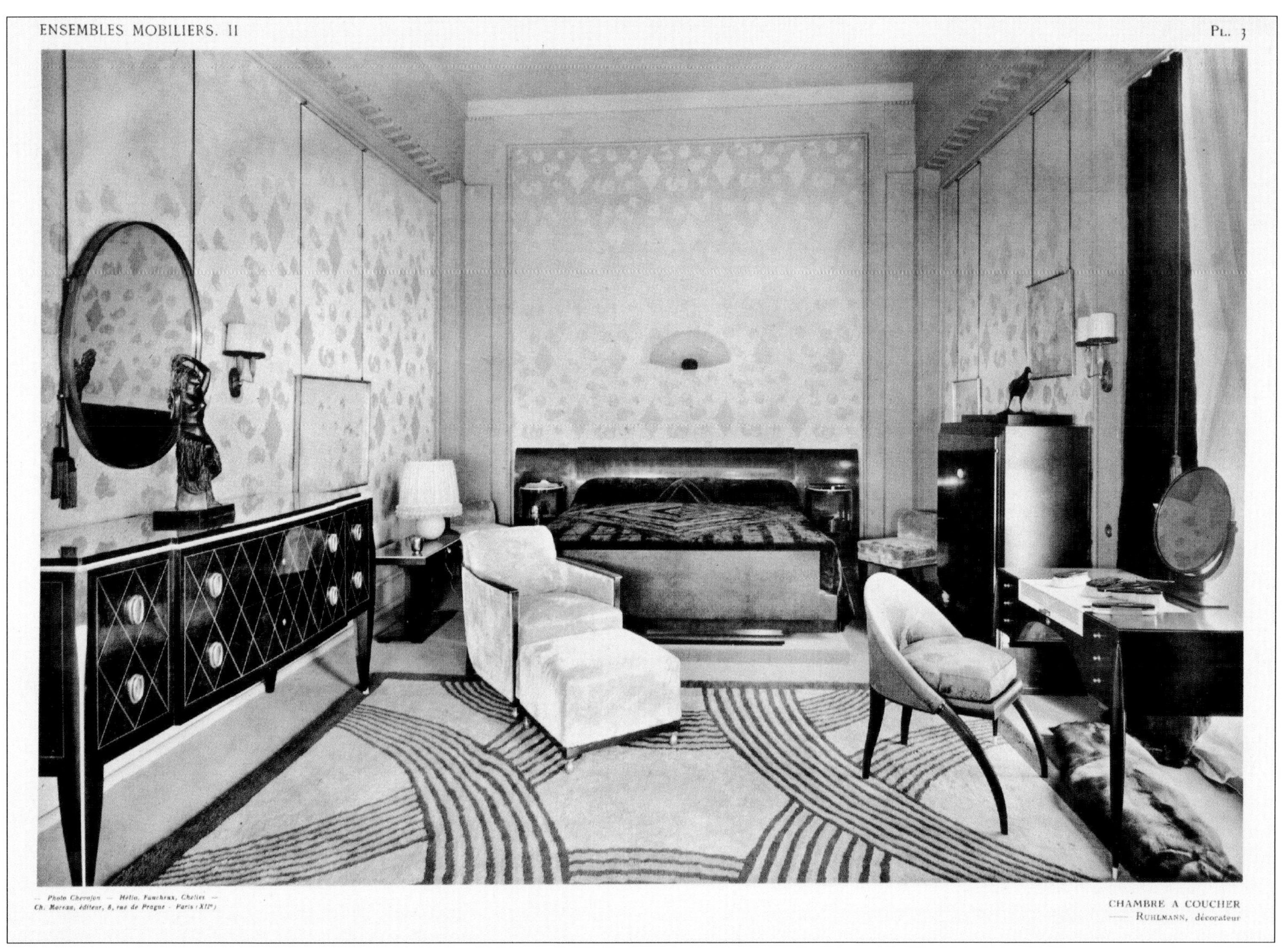

BATHER

Watercolour on paper, by René Vincent, c.1925. Chateau Musée, Dieppe, France.

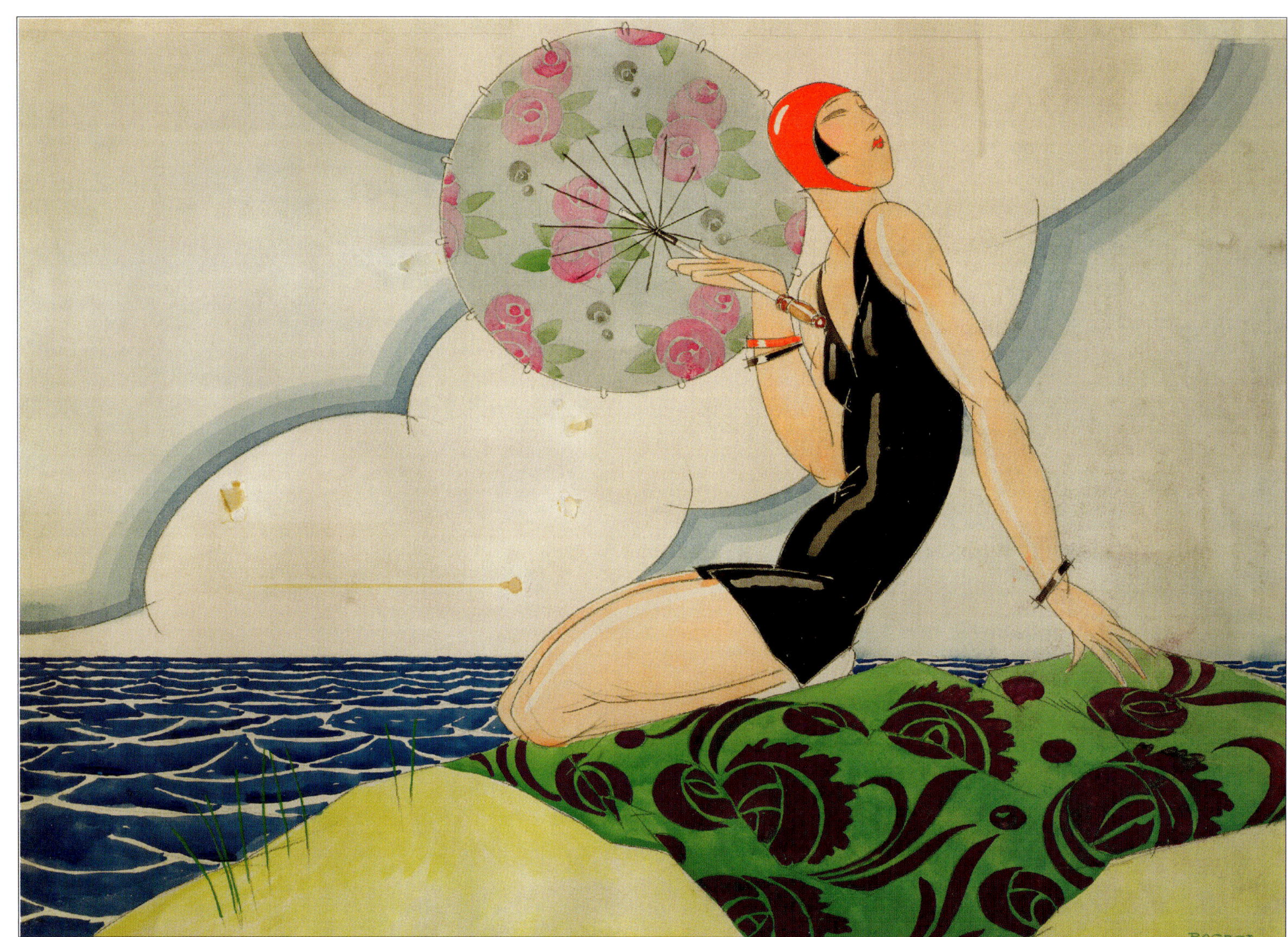

Nanking Vase

Clear and black enamel on glass, by René Jules Lalique, 1925. Private collection.

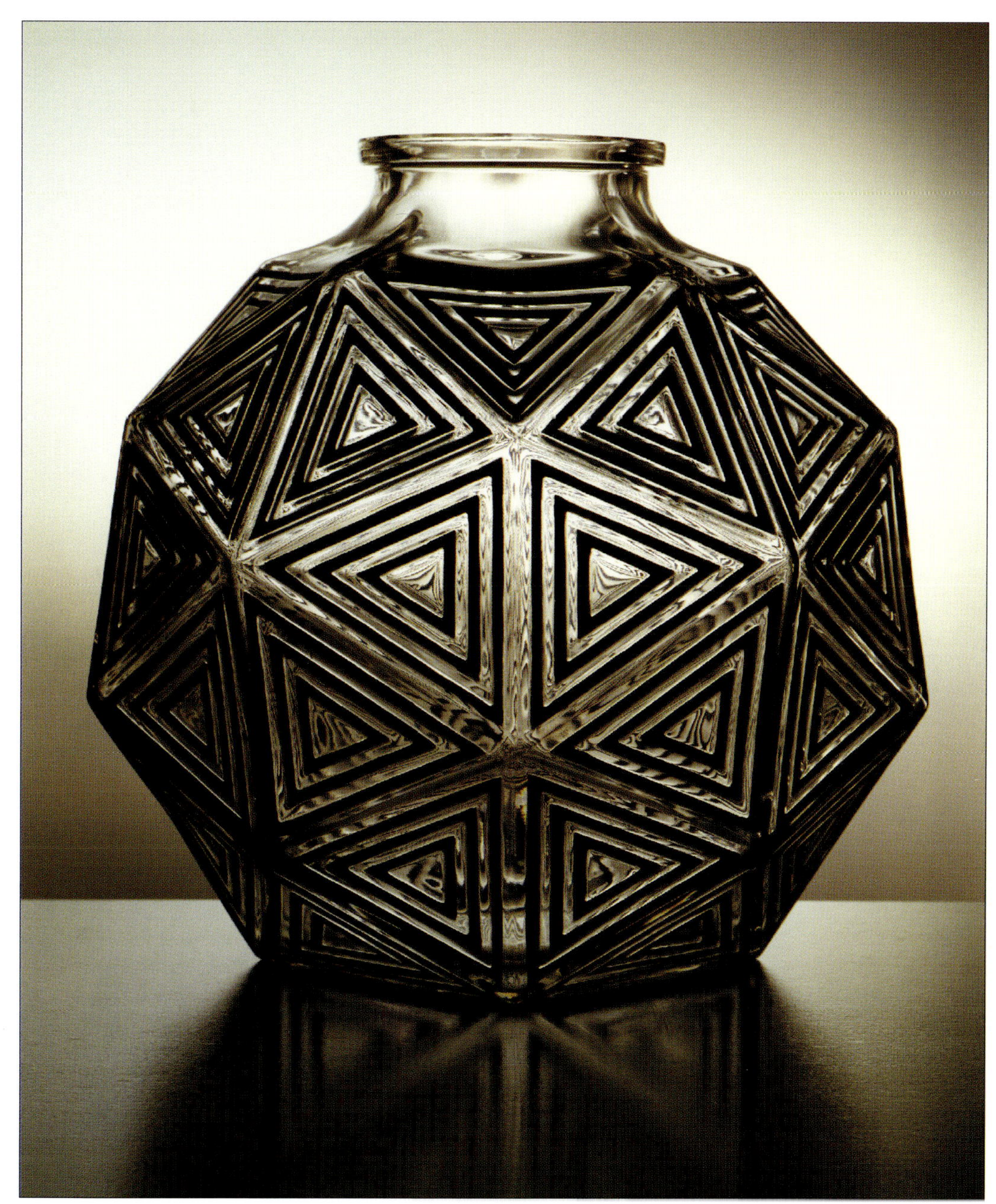

Plate 35

Office Chair

Beech, by Pierre Chareau, 1925. Musée des Arts Decoratifs, Paris, France.

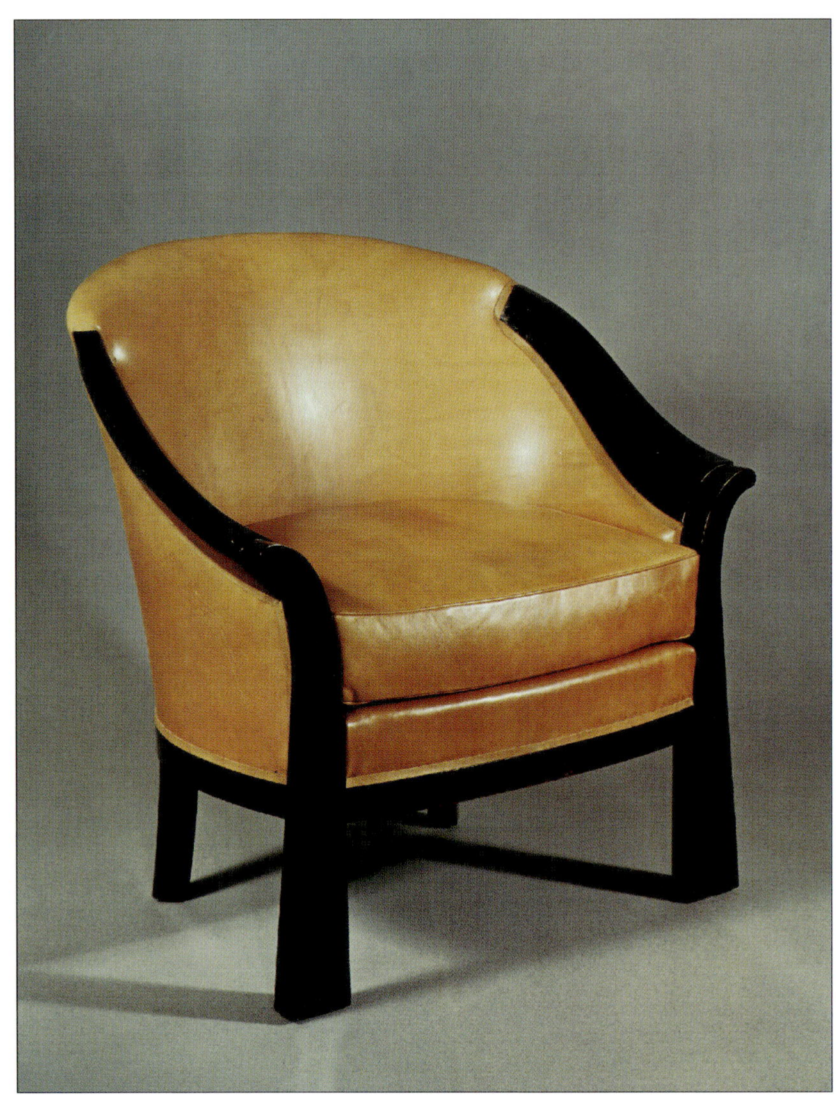

Tiffany Tea Set

Plate 36

Sterling Silver Tea Set, by Louis Comfort Tiffany, c.1920s. Private collection.

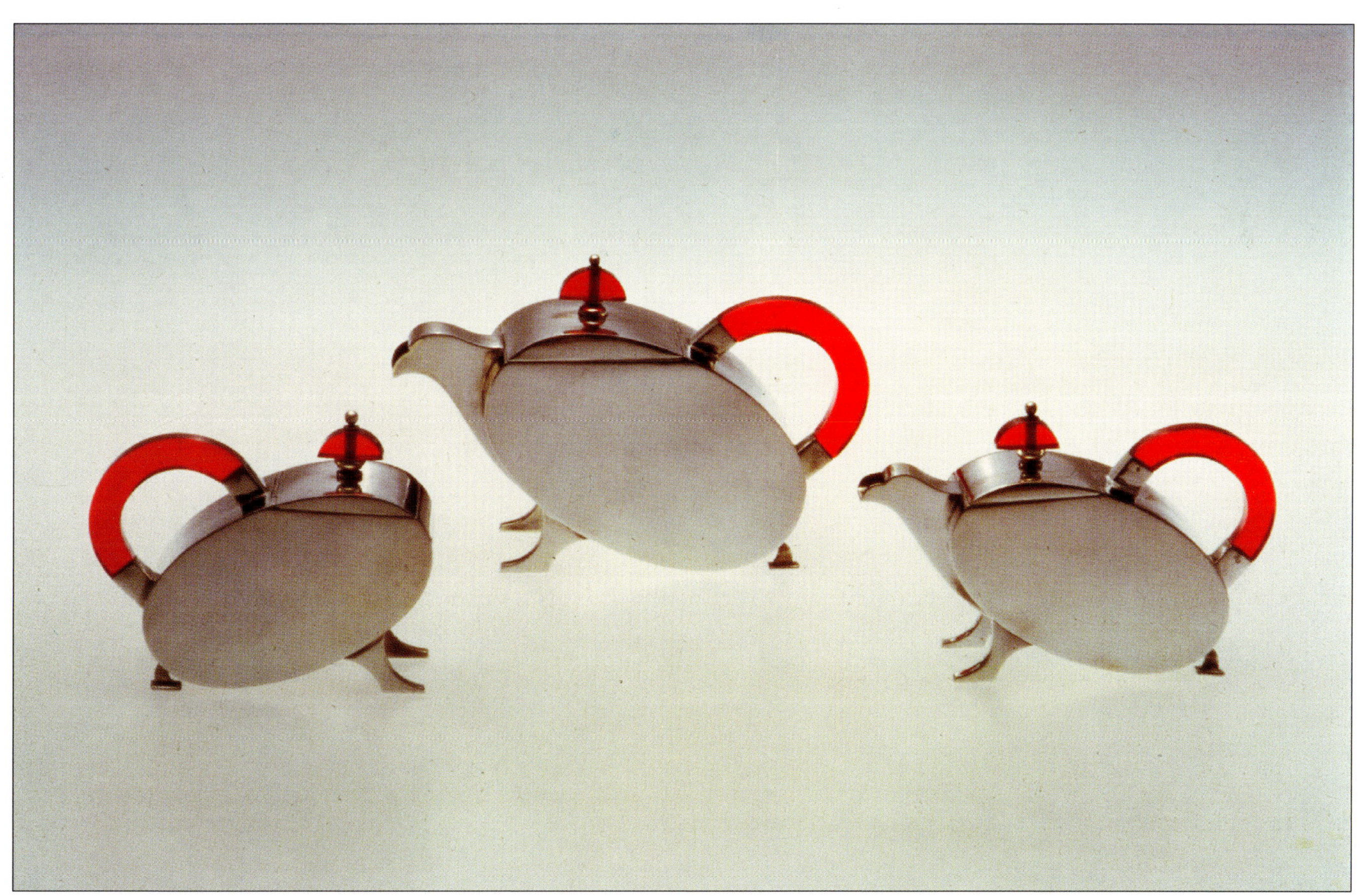

Plate 37 Ceramics from 'Repertoire du Gout Moderne'

Colour litho, by Francis Jourdain, c. 1920s.
Private collection/ The Stapleton collection.

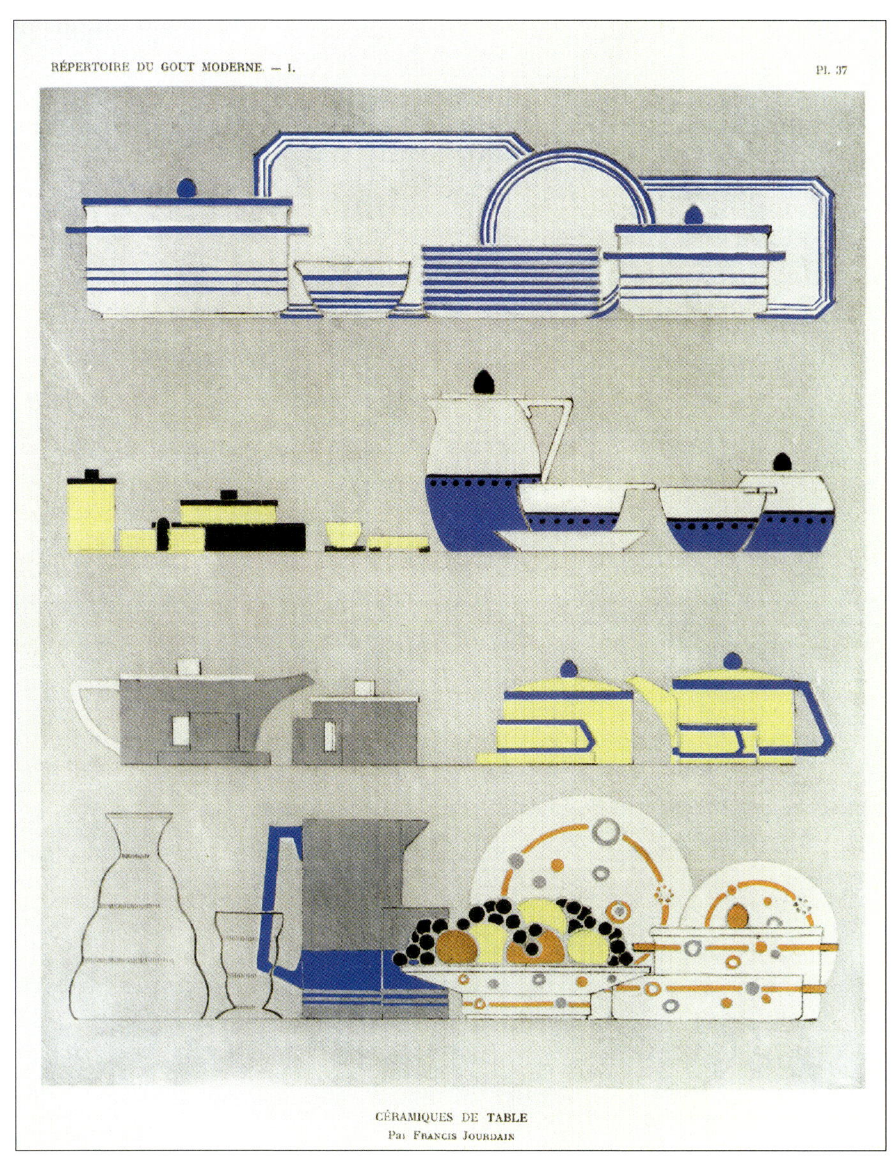

NEW YORK

Plate 38

Oil on canvas, by Tamara de Lempicka, 1925-26. Private Collection.

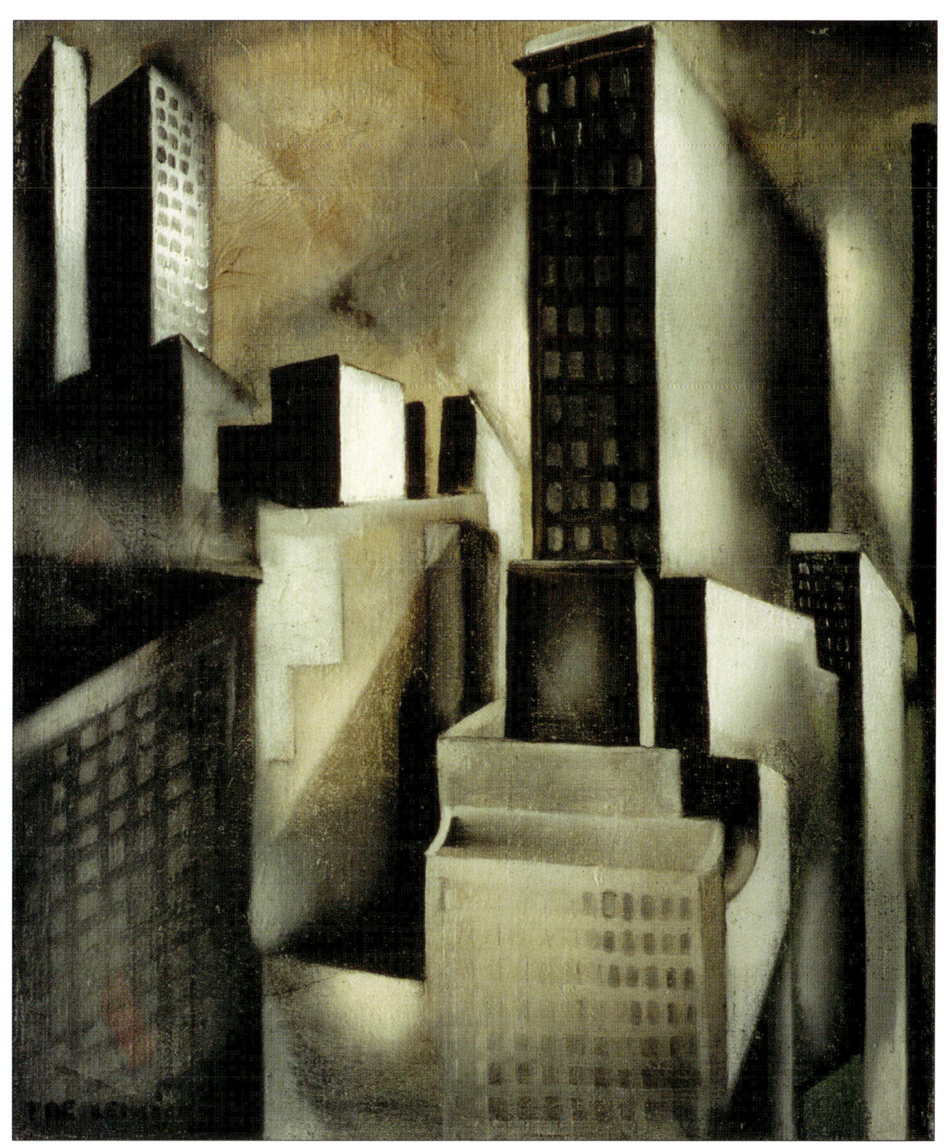

Kizette en Rose

Oil on canvas, by Tamara de Lempicka, 1926. Musée des Beaux-Arts, Nantes, France.

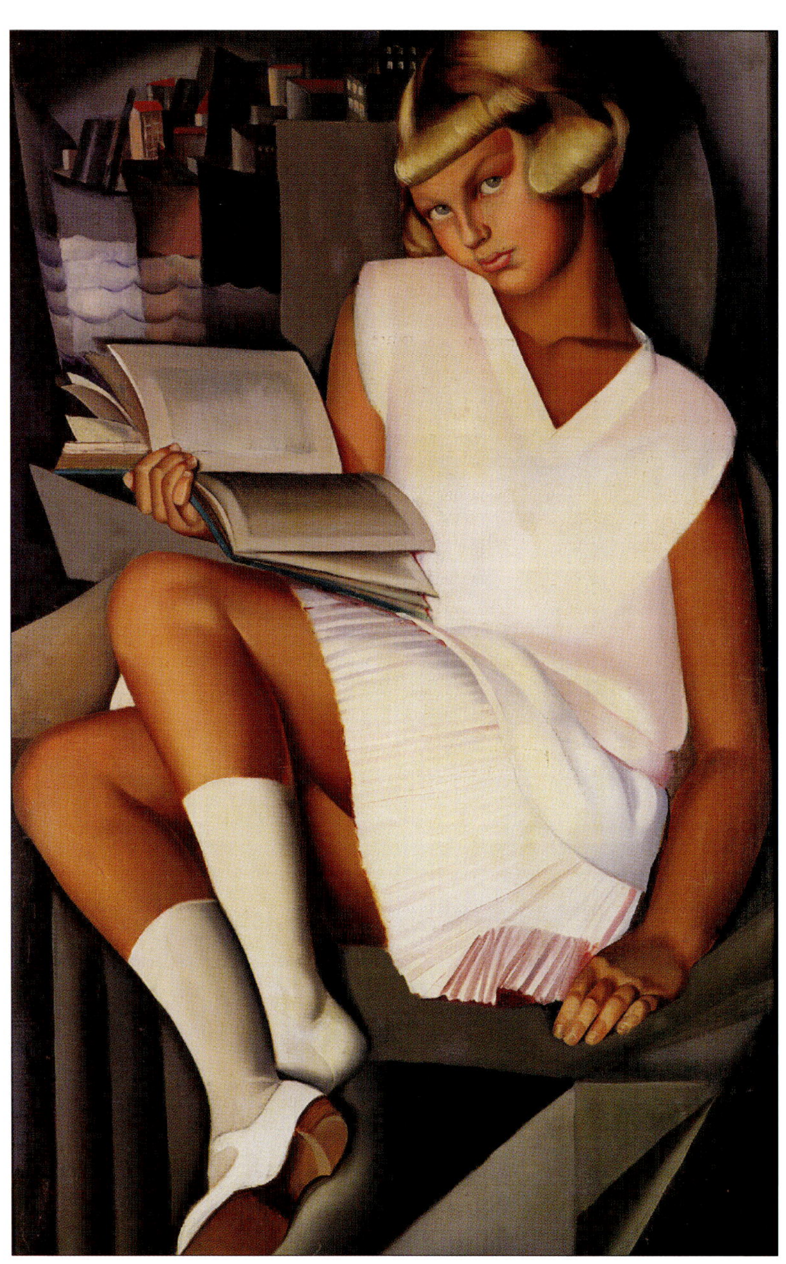

Young Girl in Green

Oil on canvas, by Tamara de Lempicka, 1927, Musée National d'Art Moderne, Centre Pompidou, Paris, France.

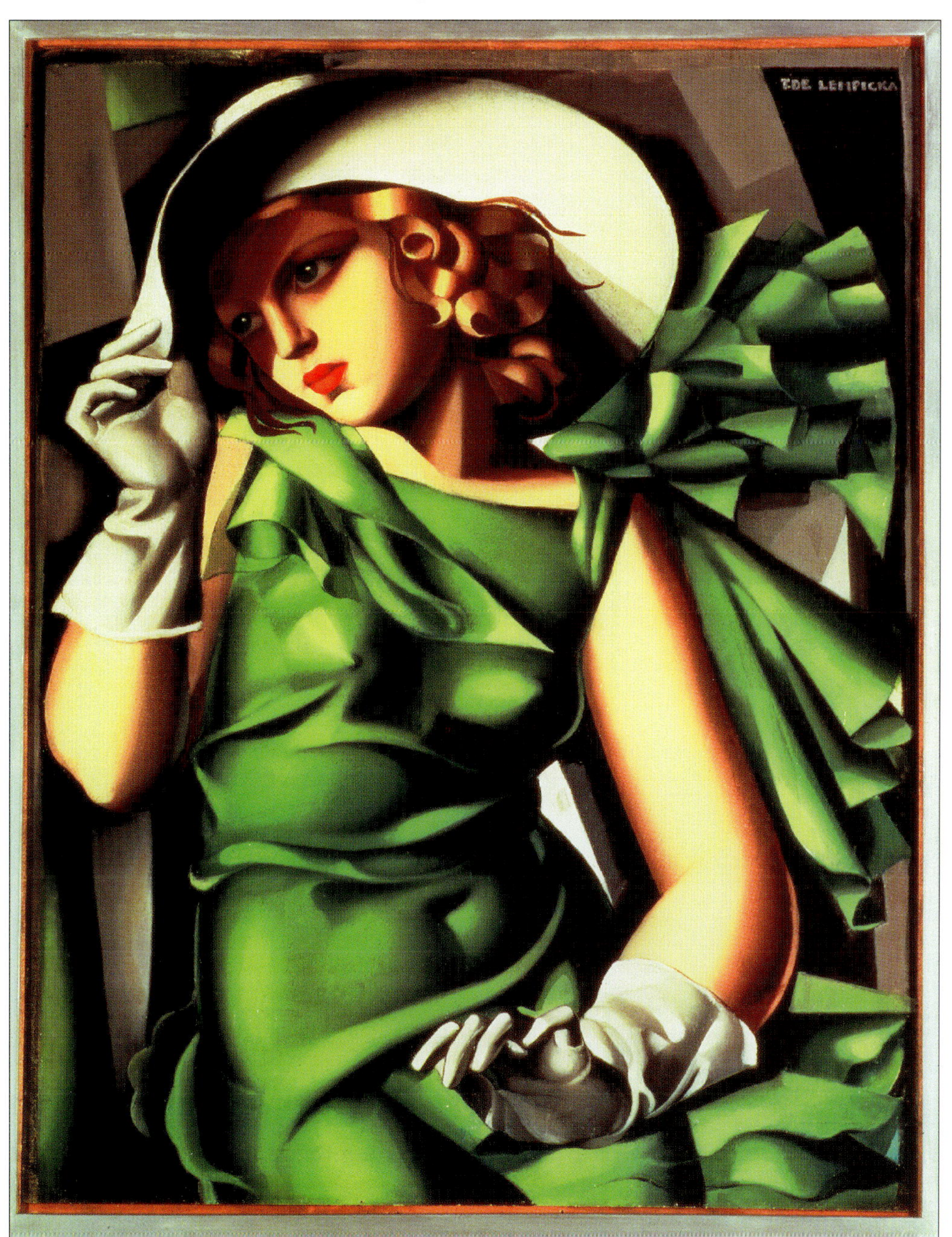

Plate 41

THE CHRYSLER BUILDING

View of the top of the pinnacle, or 'Vortex', designed by William van Alen, 1927-30.

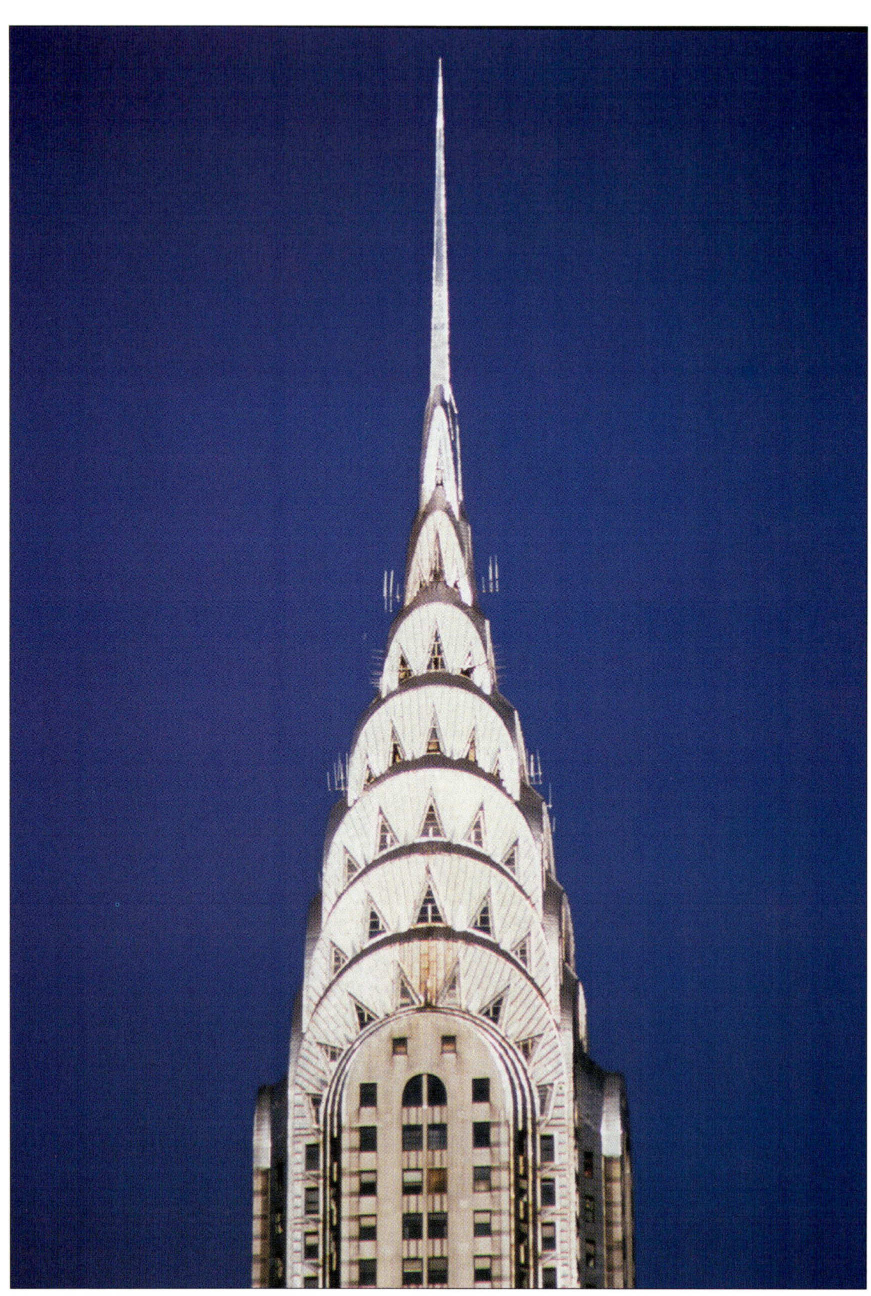

The Chrysler Building

The Chrysler Building, New York, USA
designed by William van Alen, 1927-30

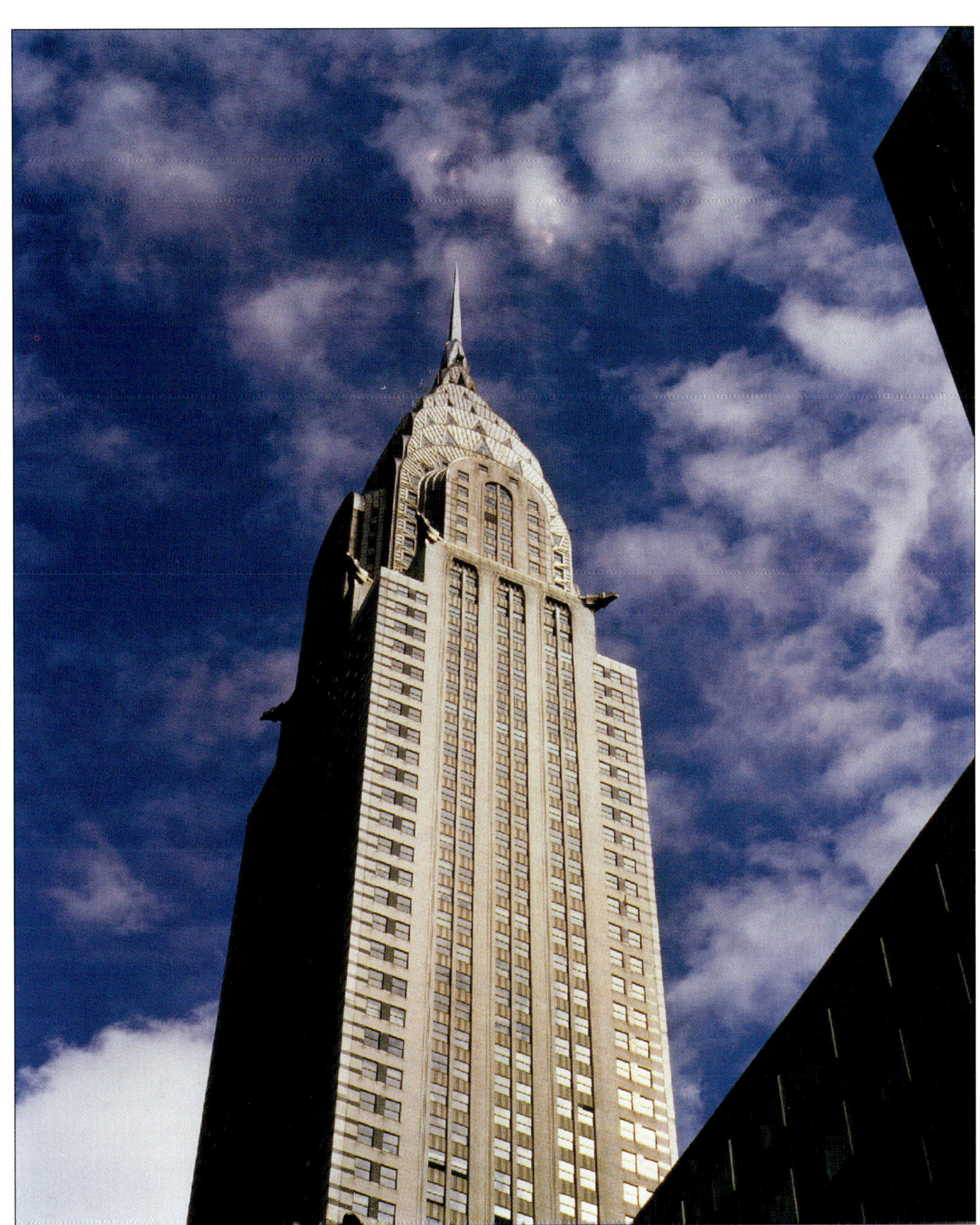

Plate 43 CAR MASCOTS, ASHTRAYS AND A PAPERWEIGHT

Glass object d'art by René Jules Lalique, c.1928. Private collection.

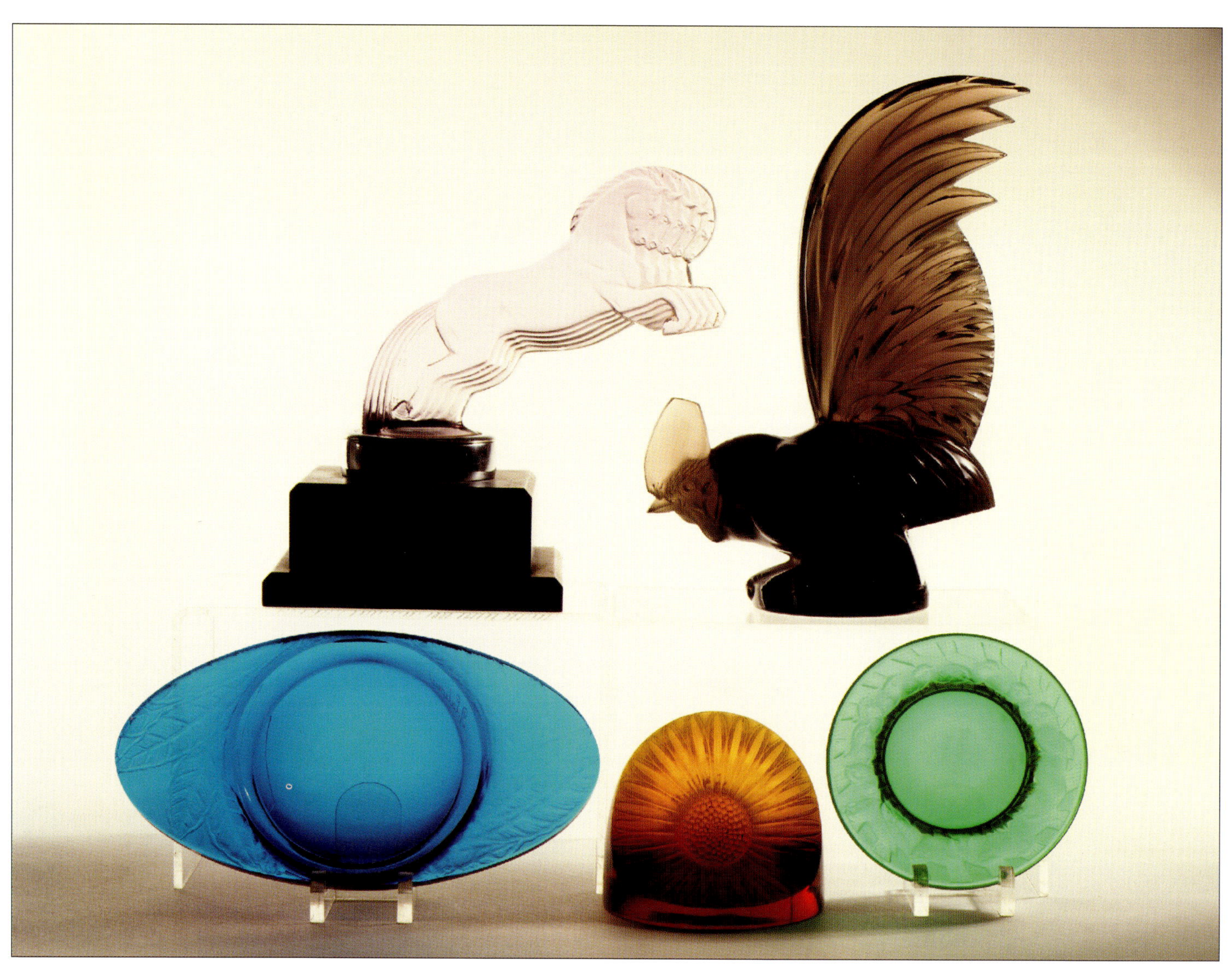

Golfers

Ceramic tile panel, artist unknown, c.1920s.
Private collection/ Wingfield Sporting Gallery, London, UK.

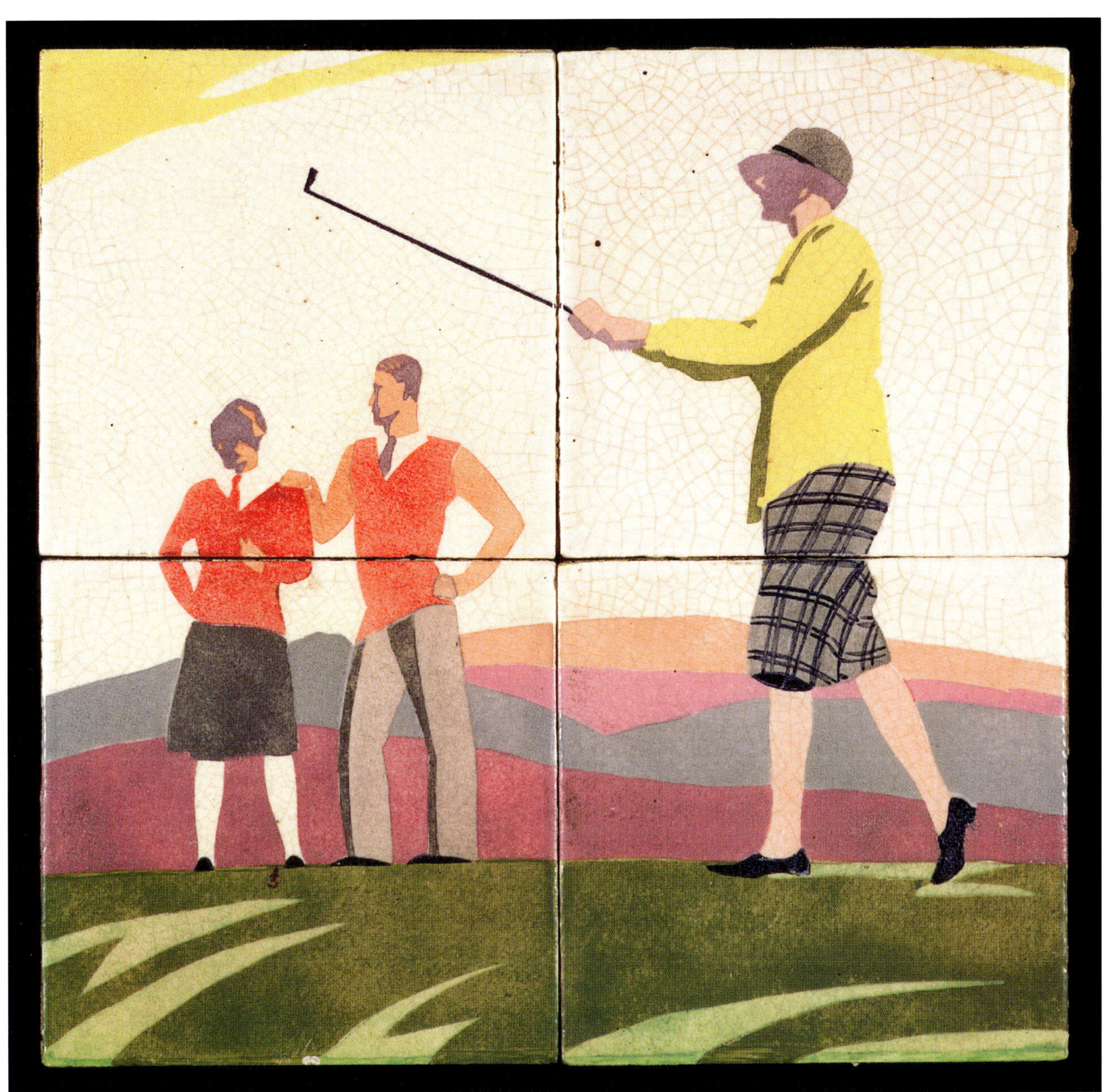

ETABLISSEMENTS CITROEN

Avenue des Champs- Elysees, exposition hall (interior), Ravazi Boutiques, Editions S de Bonadona, Paris, designed by Henry Delacroix, late 1920s.

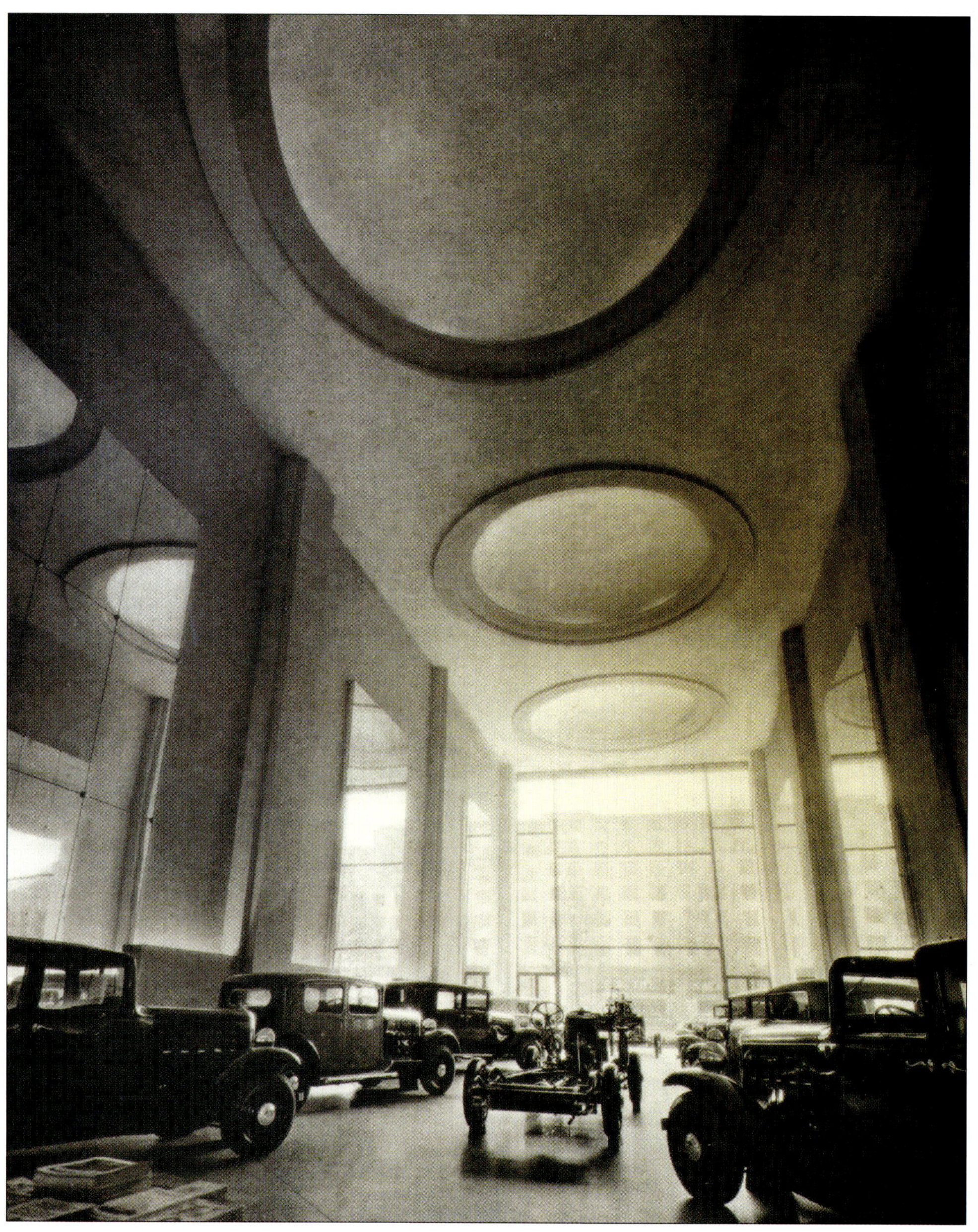

Optique Medicale

Plate 46

Optique Medicale Boutique, Paris, facade in black glass, by Jean Revenel, c. late 1920s. Pochoir print. Private collection.

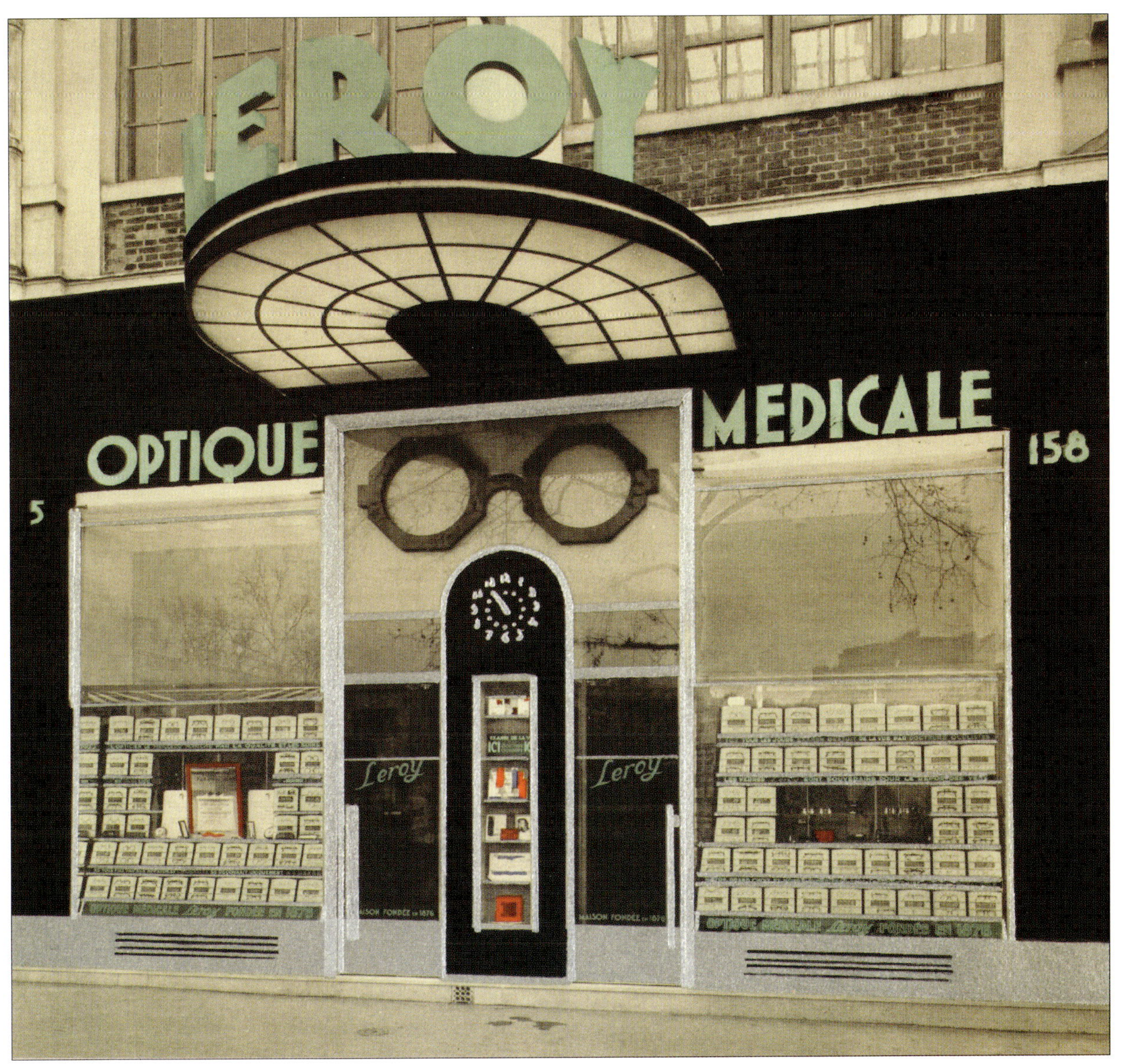

Plate 47

'Grande Libellule' Car Mascot

Amethyst frosted glass car mascot, by René Jules Lalique, c. 1929.
Private collection.

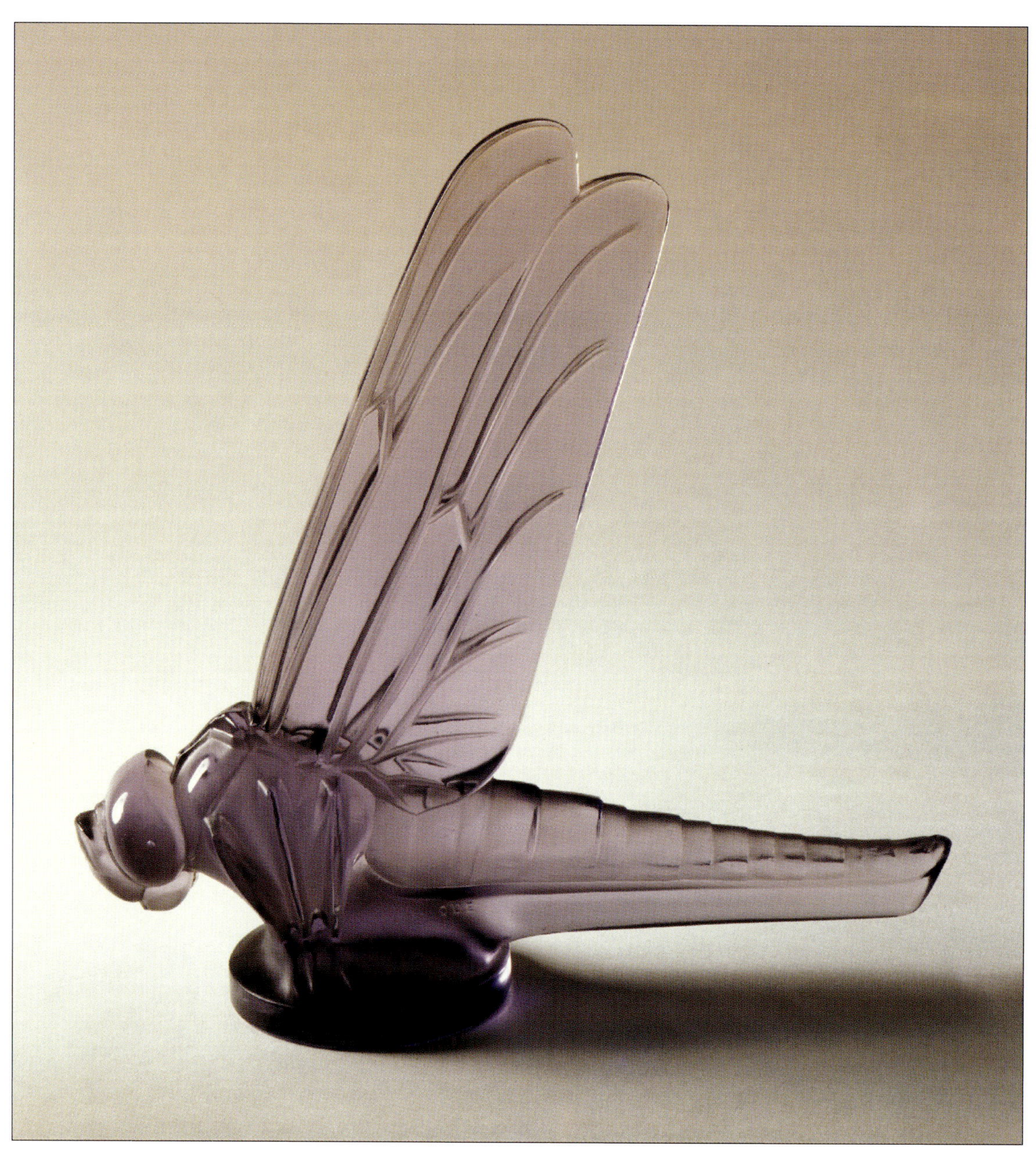

Scent Bottles

Plate 48

A selection of glass scent bottles, by René Jules Lalique, c. 1929. Private collection.

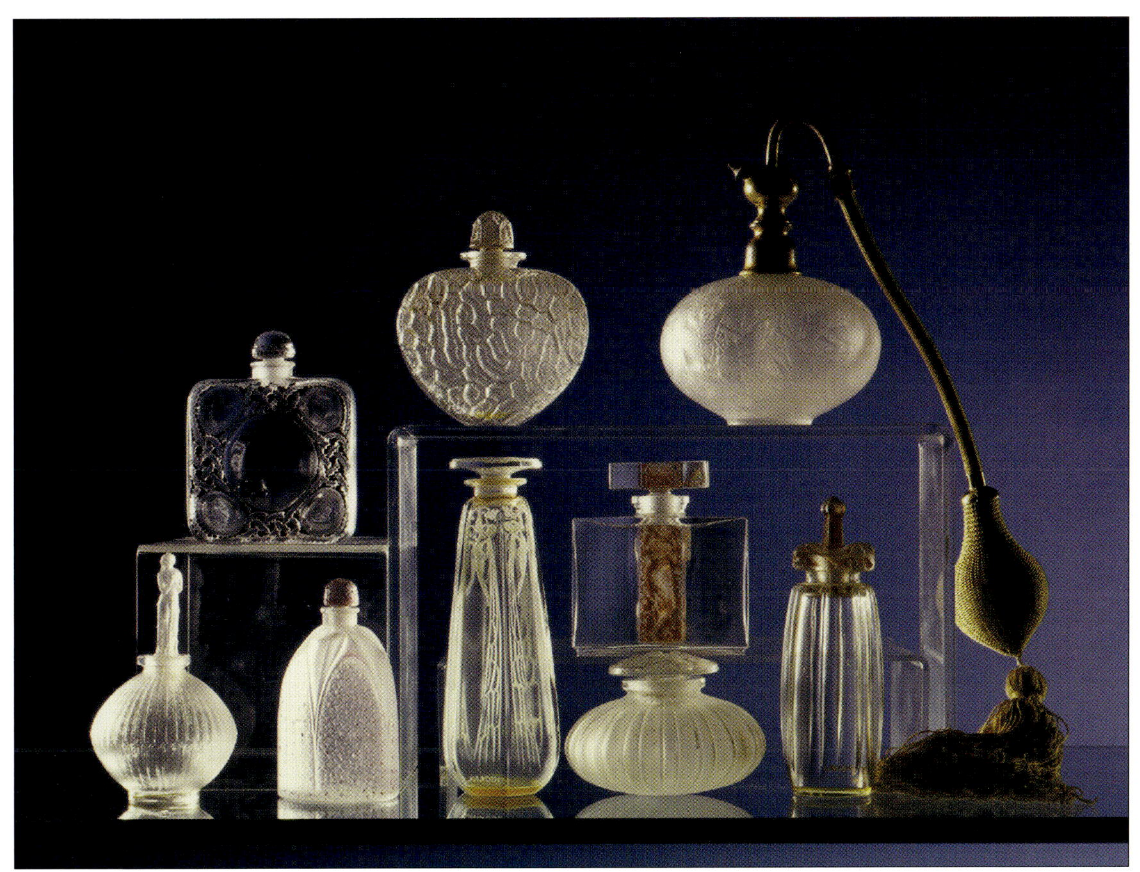

Plate 49

Radiator Grill

Radiator Grill for the Chanin Building, New York, USA, by Jacques Delamarre, c. 1929.

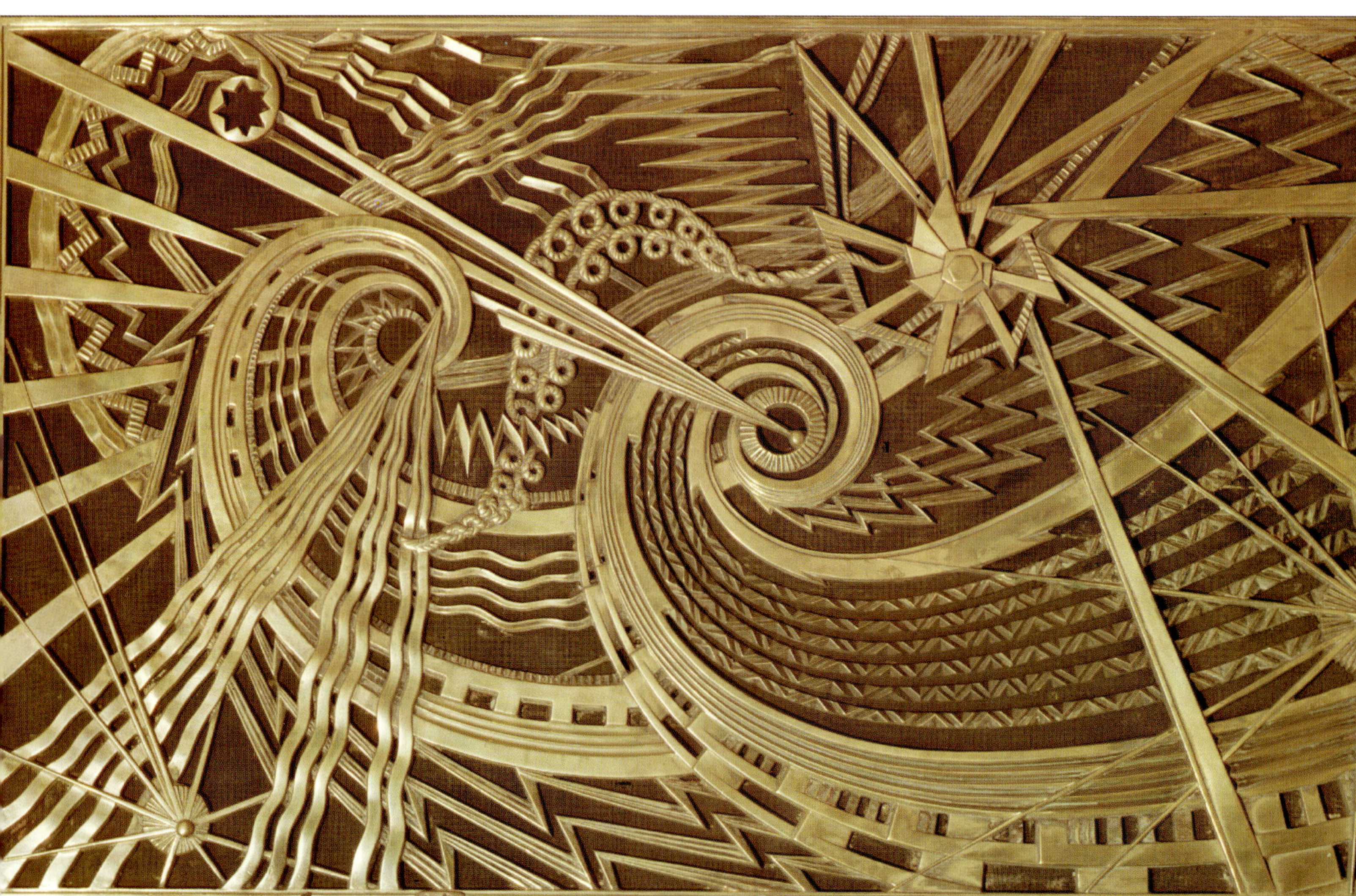

Dragonfly Car Mascot

Sabino opalescent glass, by unknown artist, c.1929. Private collection.

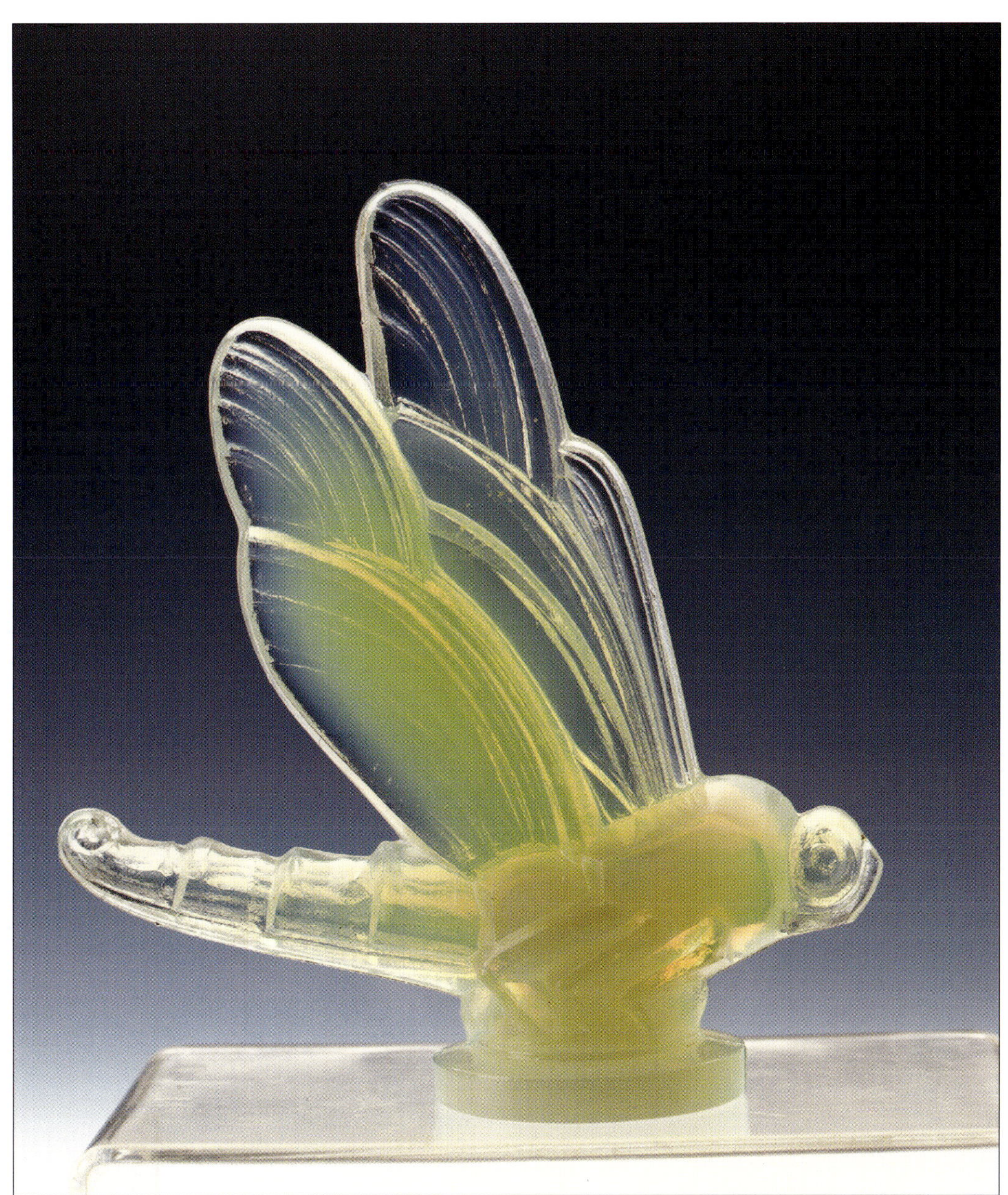

Plate 51 'Sunray' Vase, Teapot and Coffee Pot

Ceramic 'Sunray' pattern vase, conical teapot and coffee pot by Clarice Cliff, 1929-30. Private collection.

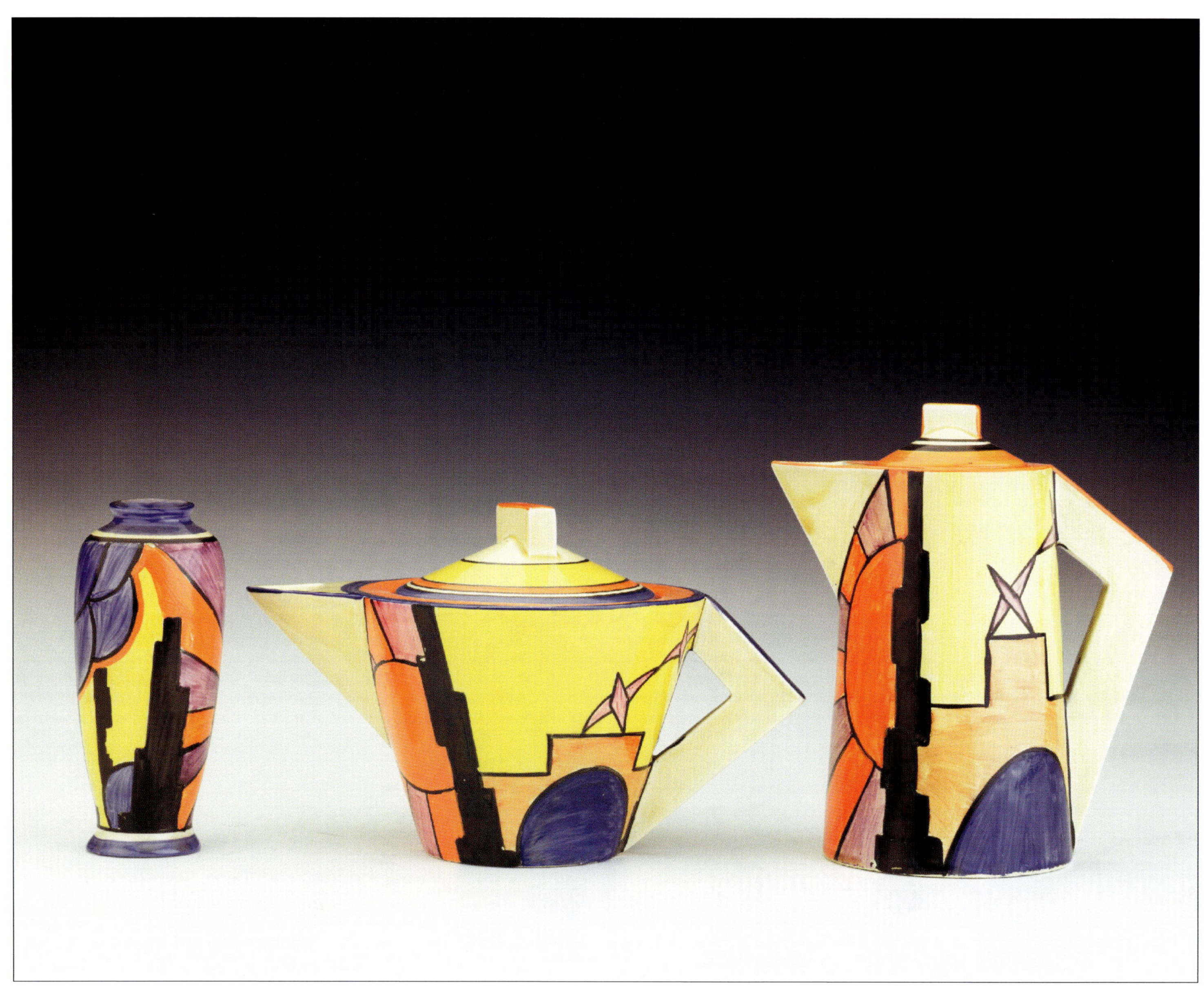

Selection of Vases

Plate 52

Glass, by René Jules Lalique, c. 1930. Private collection.

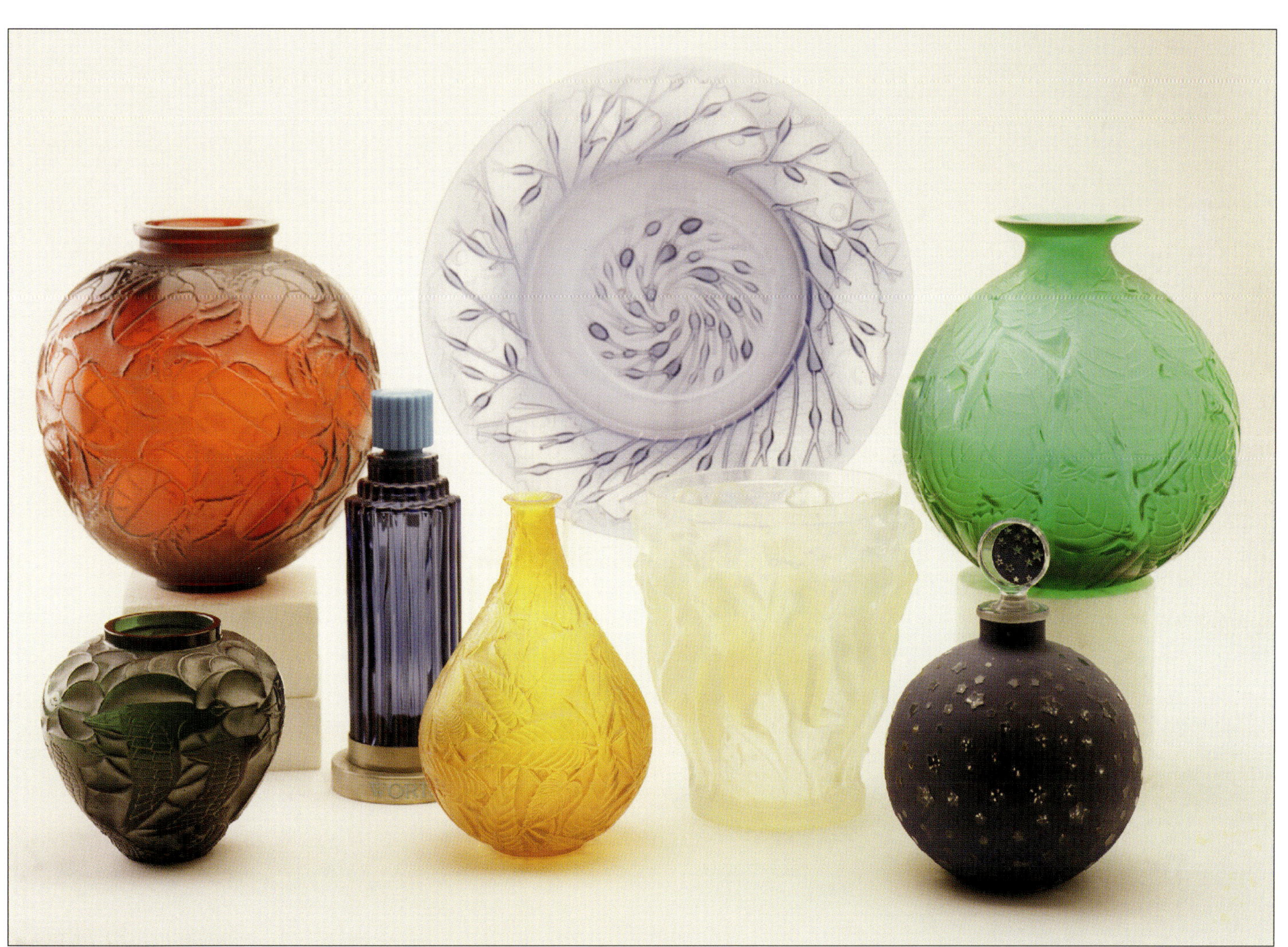

Cabinet

Birdseye maple and steel, by unknown artist, German School, c.1930.
Indianapolis Museum of Art, USA..

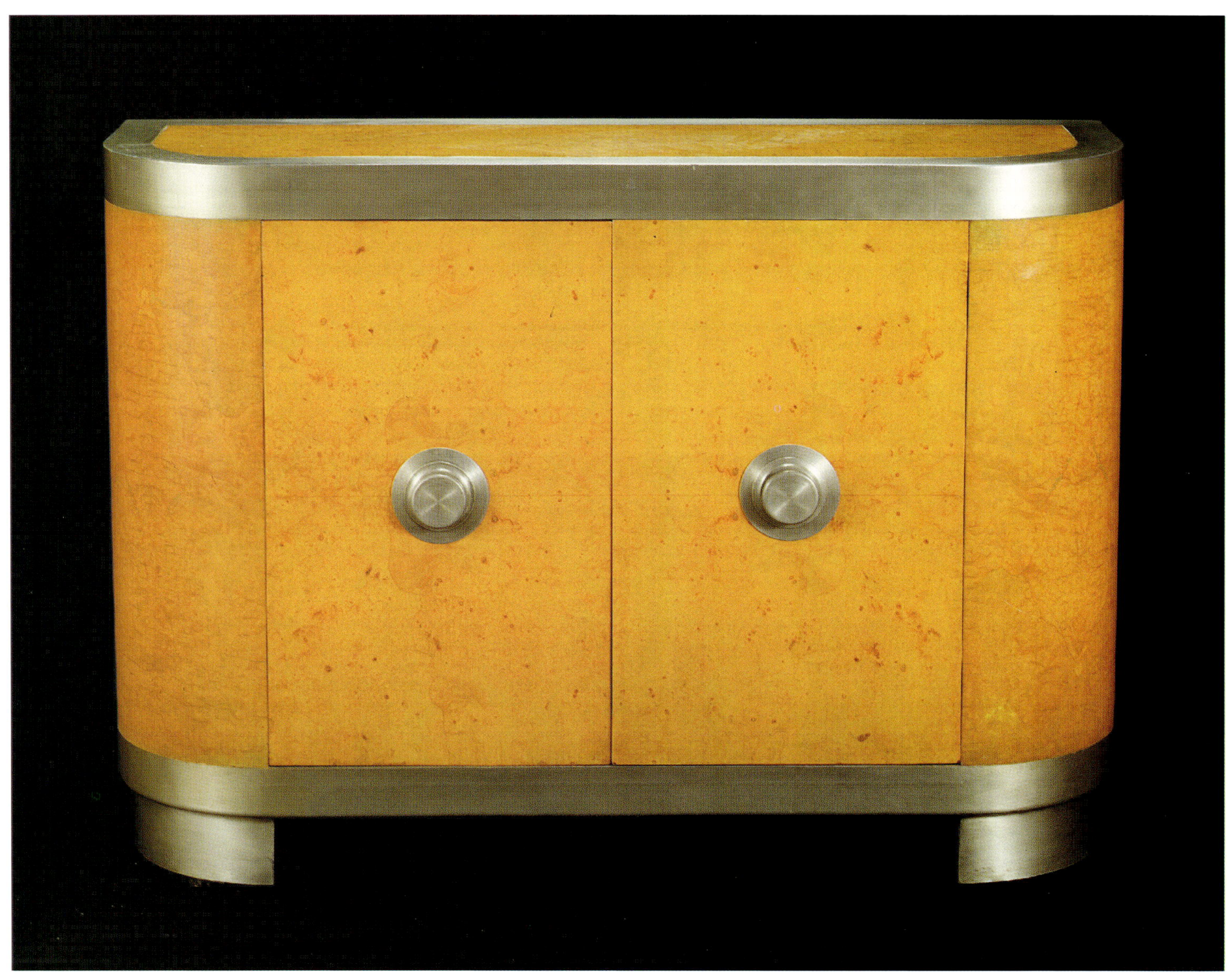

'Bizarre' Series of Ceramics

Plate 54

Ceramics, by Clarice Cliff, c.1930. Private collection.

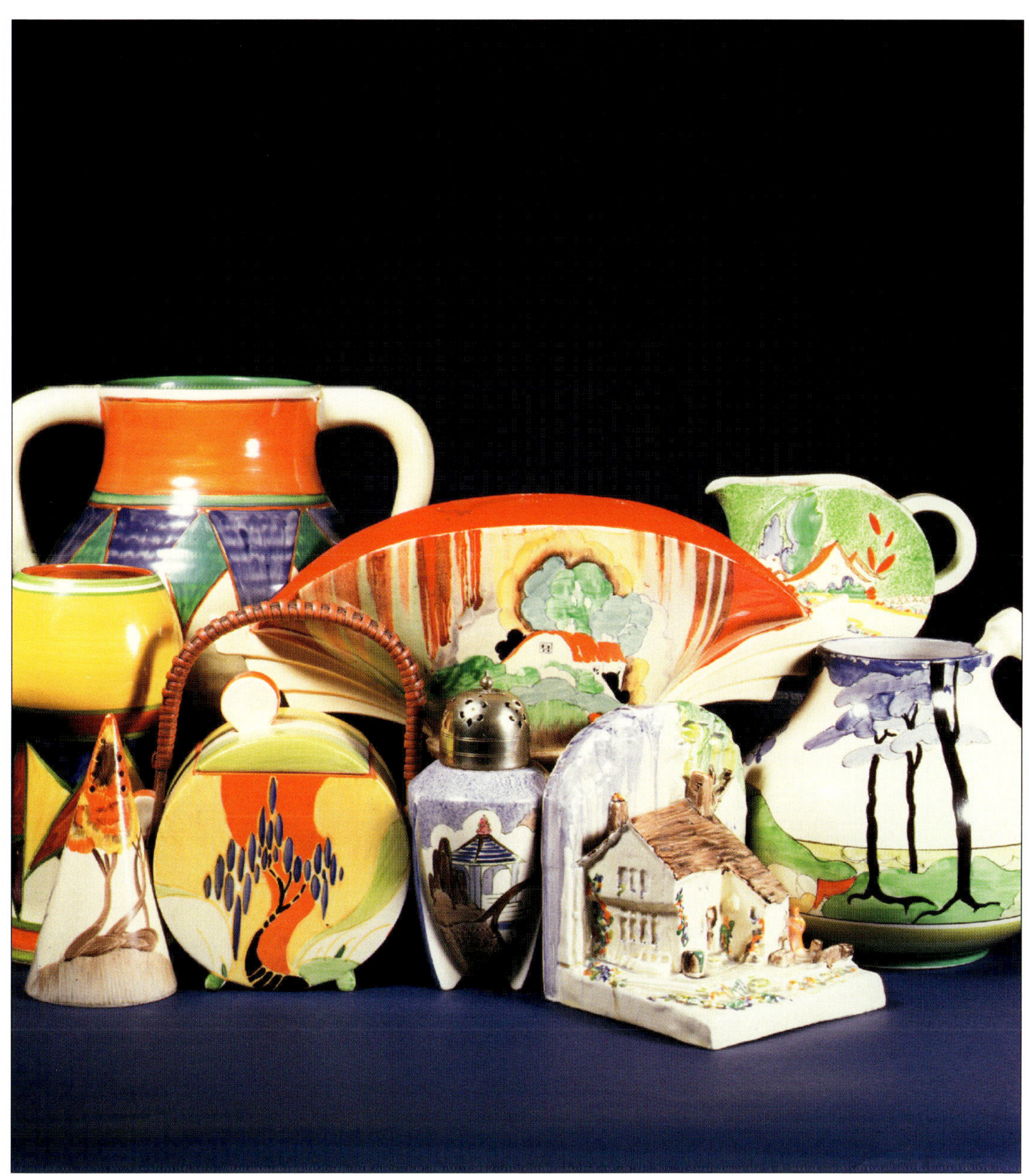

Plate 10 from *Relais* (Relay)

by Edouard Benedictus, 1930, Published by Calmann & King, London.

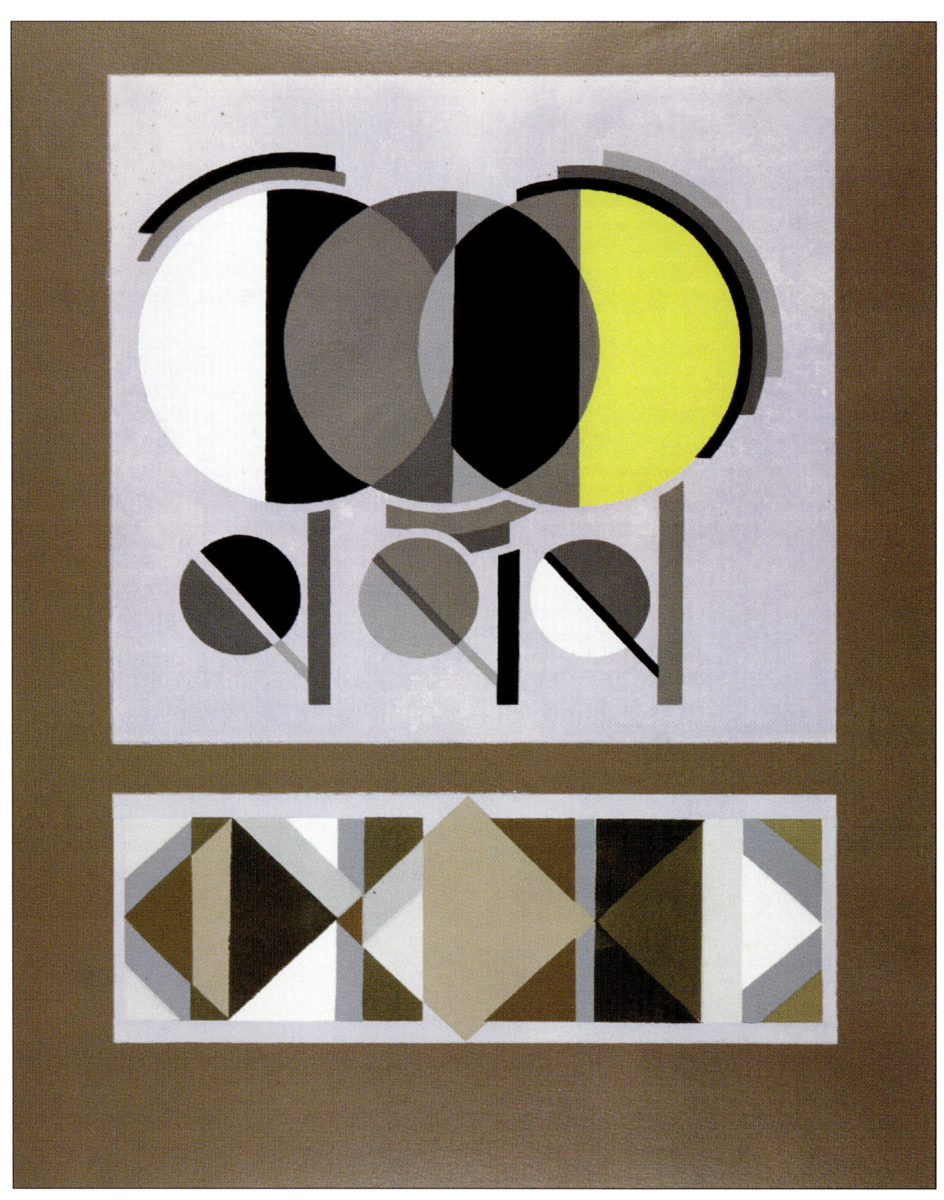

THE EMPIRE STATE BUILDING

Plate 56

Designed by William Lamb, of Shreve, Lamb & Harmon, c. 1930. Photograph © Museum of City of New York, USA.

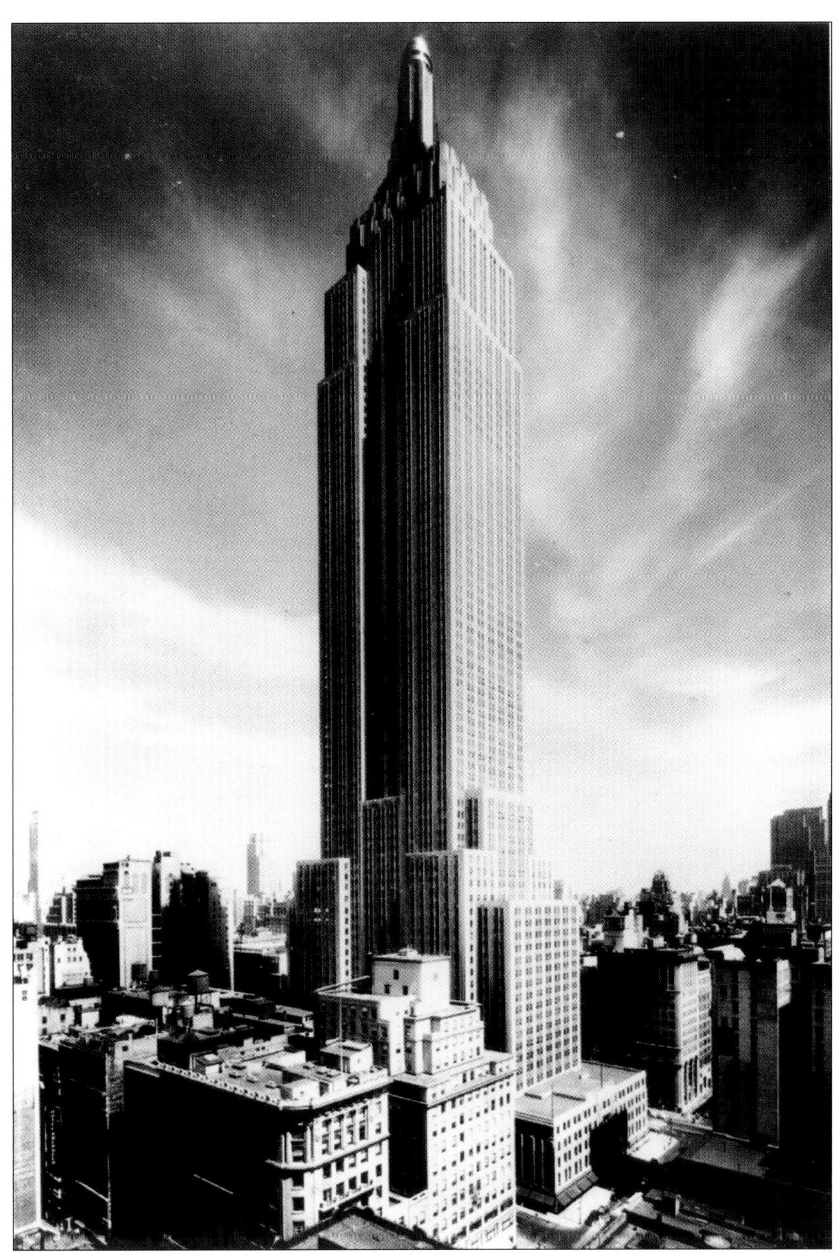

Plate 57

Teapot

Ceramic teapot, by Susie Cooper for Crown Works, Burslem c.1930.
Private Collection.

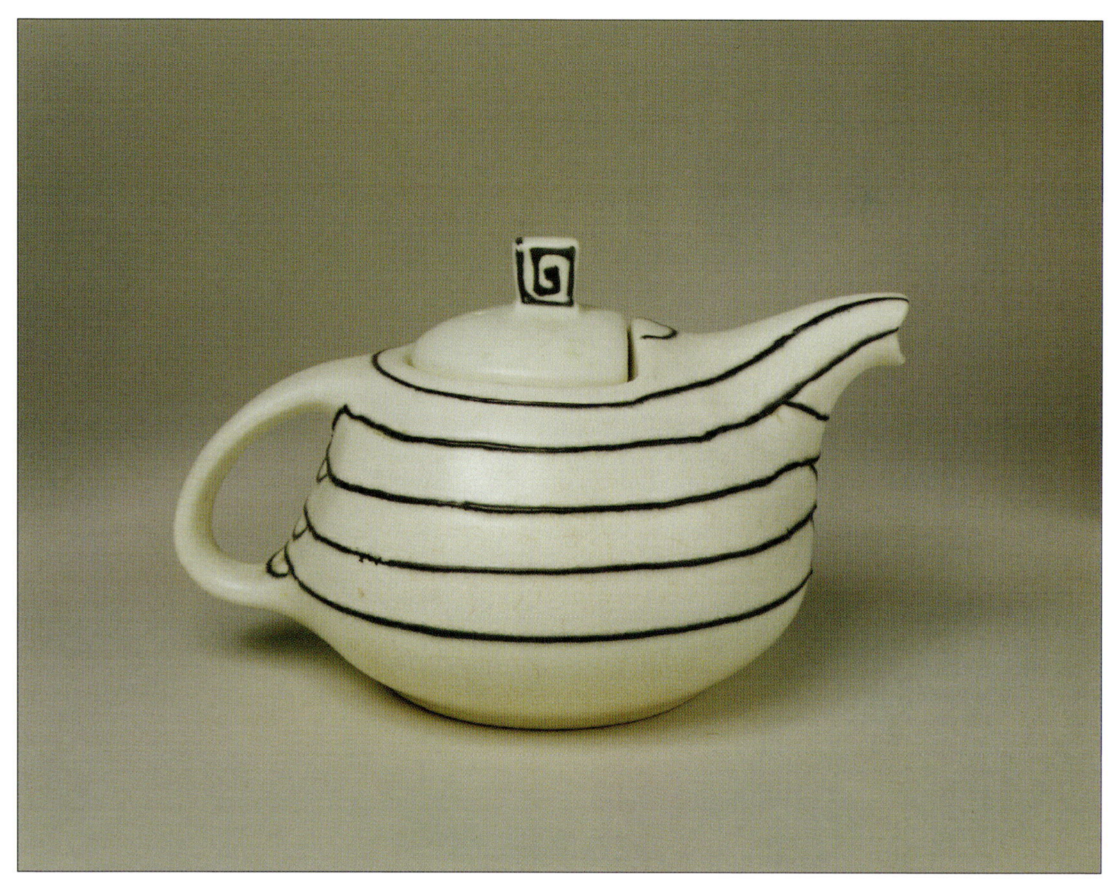

'Suzanne au Bain'

Plate 58

Opalescent glass statuette, by René Jules Lalique, c. 1930. Private collection.

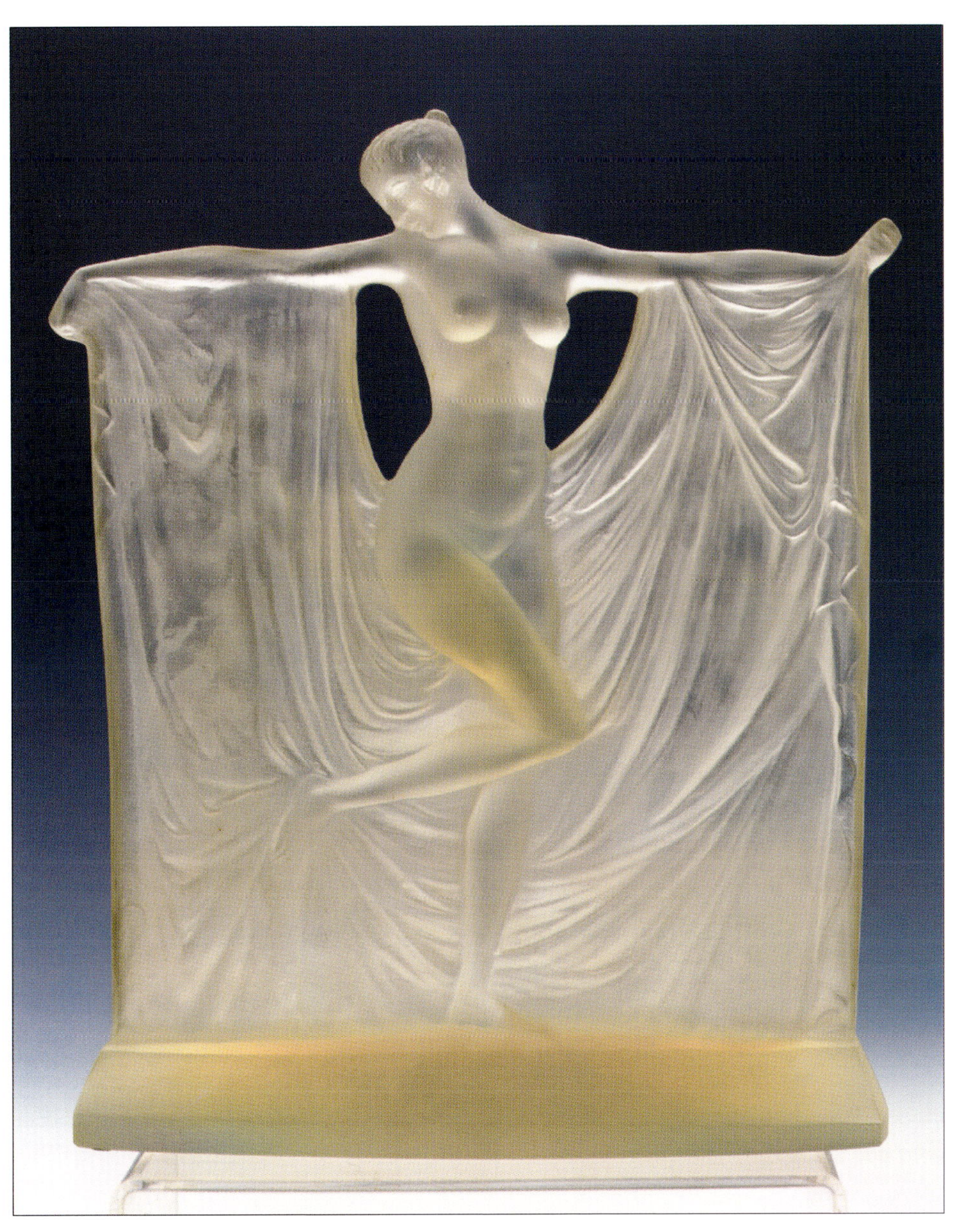

Plate 59 POSTER ADVERTISING ORIENT CRUISES

Colour litho, by Andrew Johnson, 1930. Private collection.

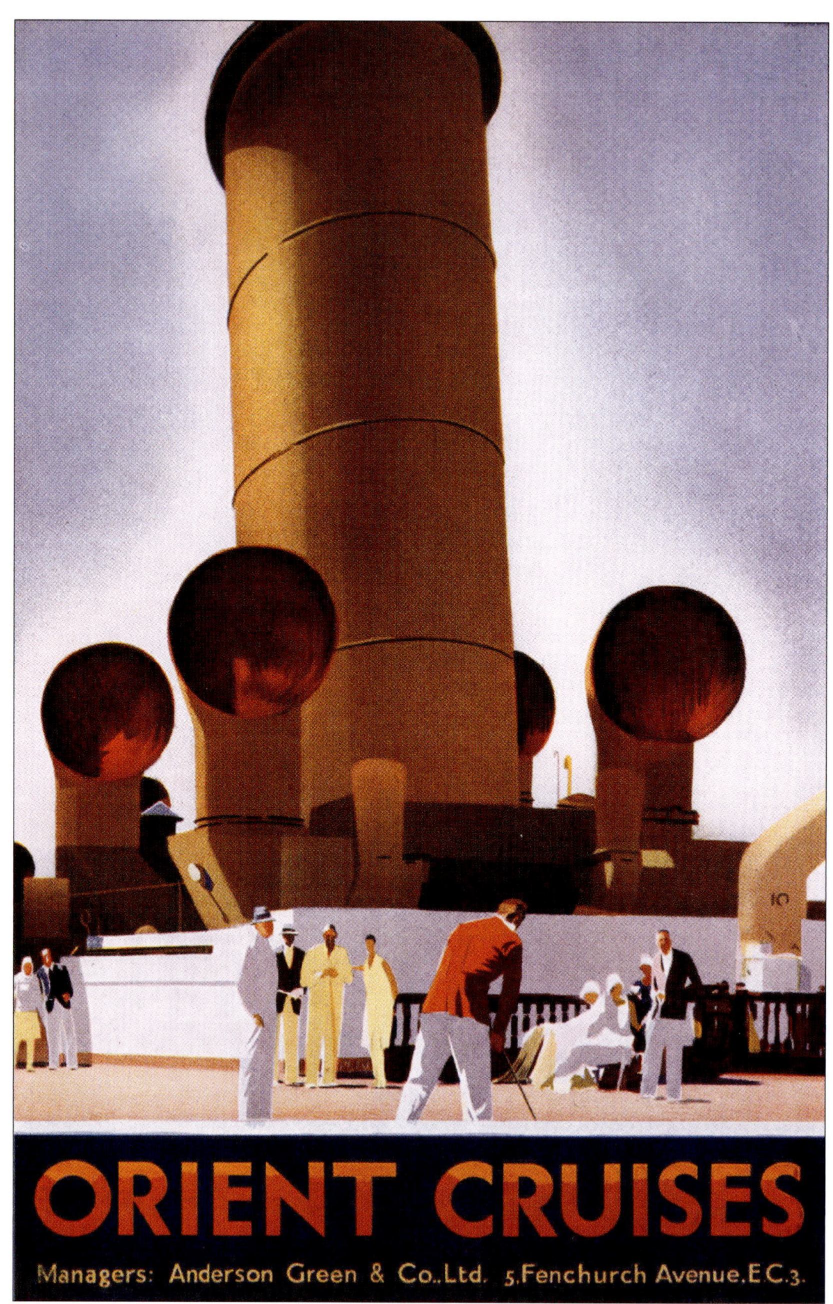

Watercolour on paper, by Janet Clark, c.1930. © The Design Library, New York, USA

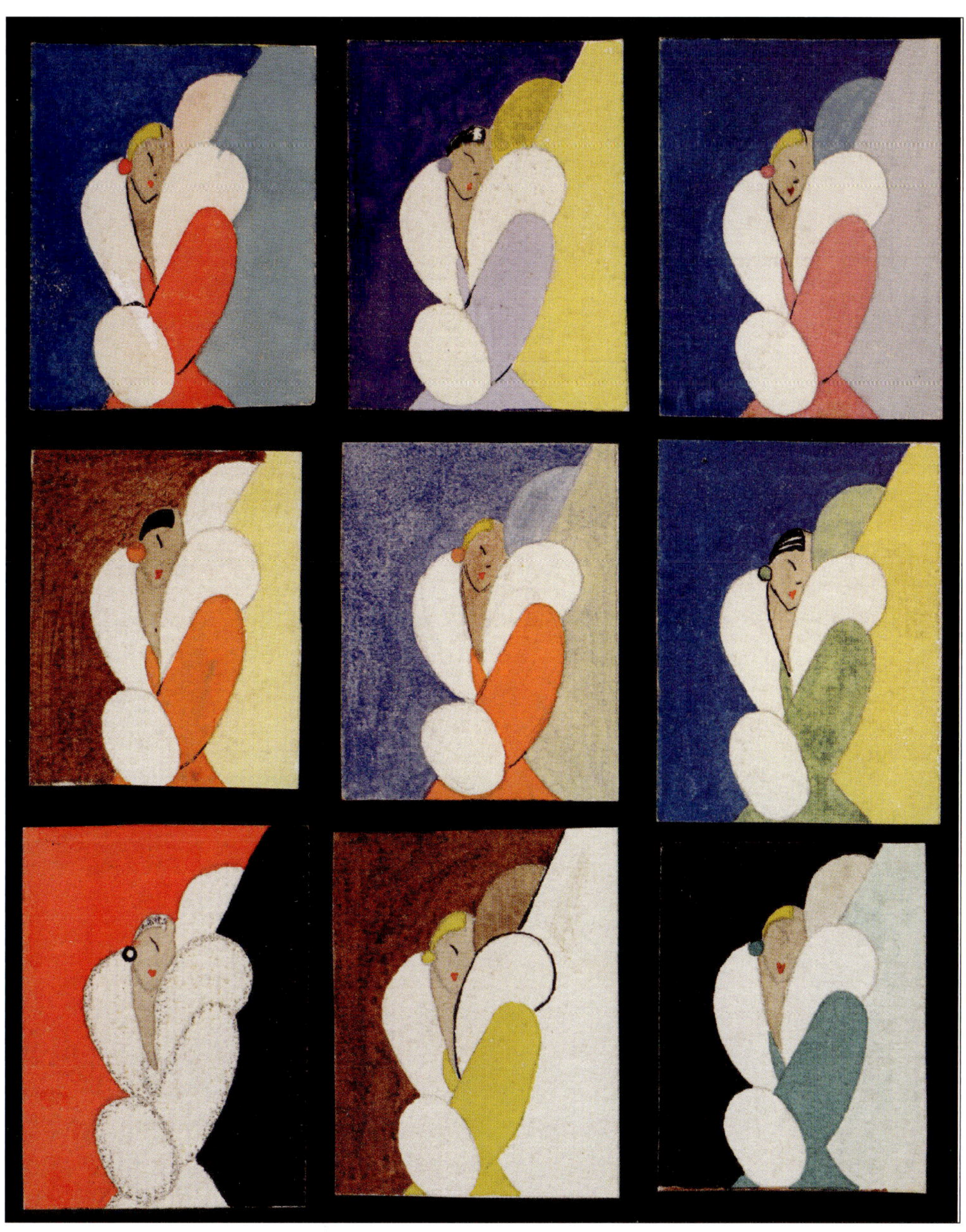

Plate 61

LUGGAGE TICKET

for the Cunard Line. Colour litho, artist unkown, c. 1930. Private collection.

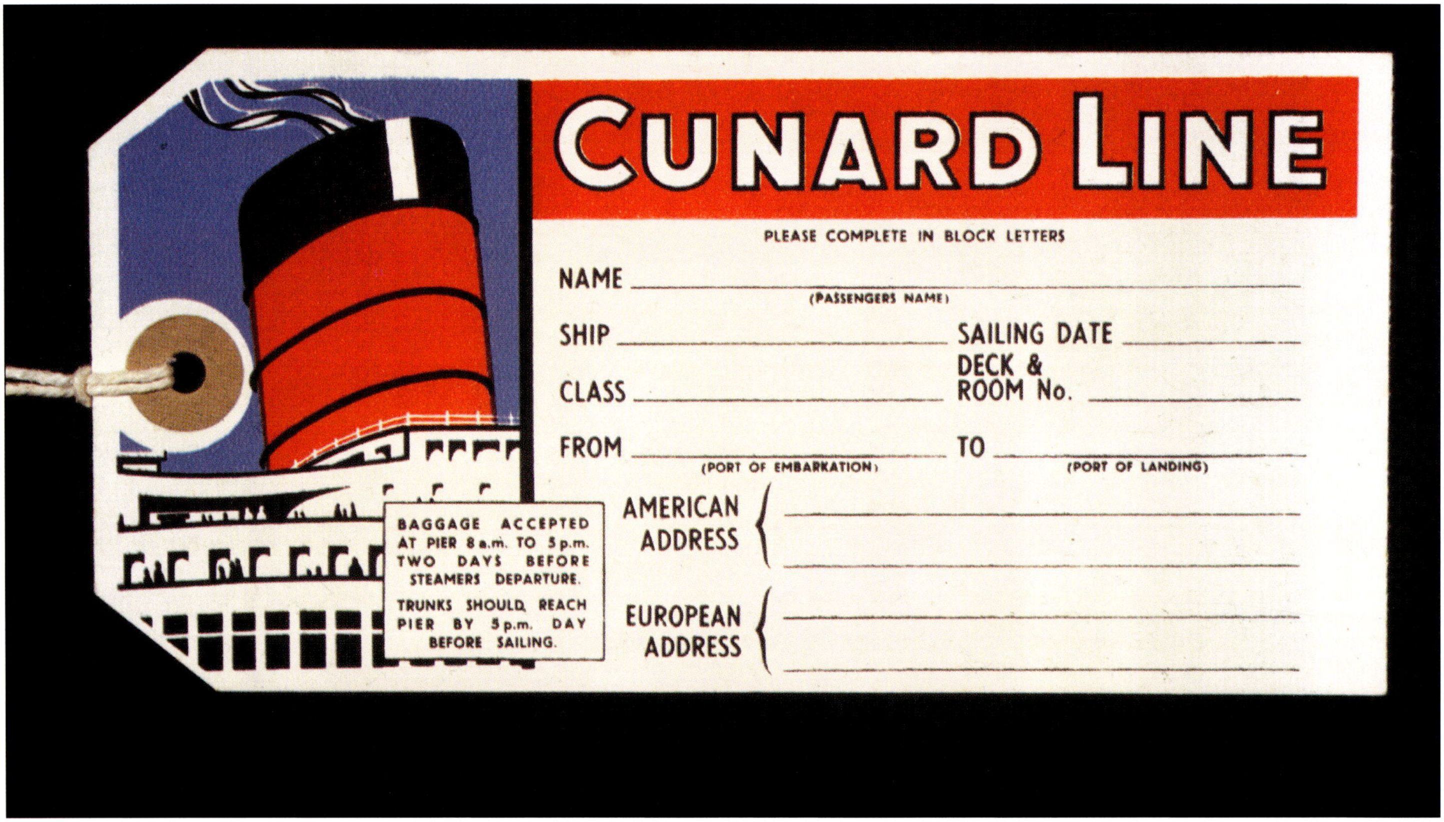

Butterfly

Pink and purple enamel butterfly, artist unknown, c.1930. Private collection.

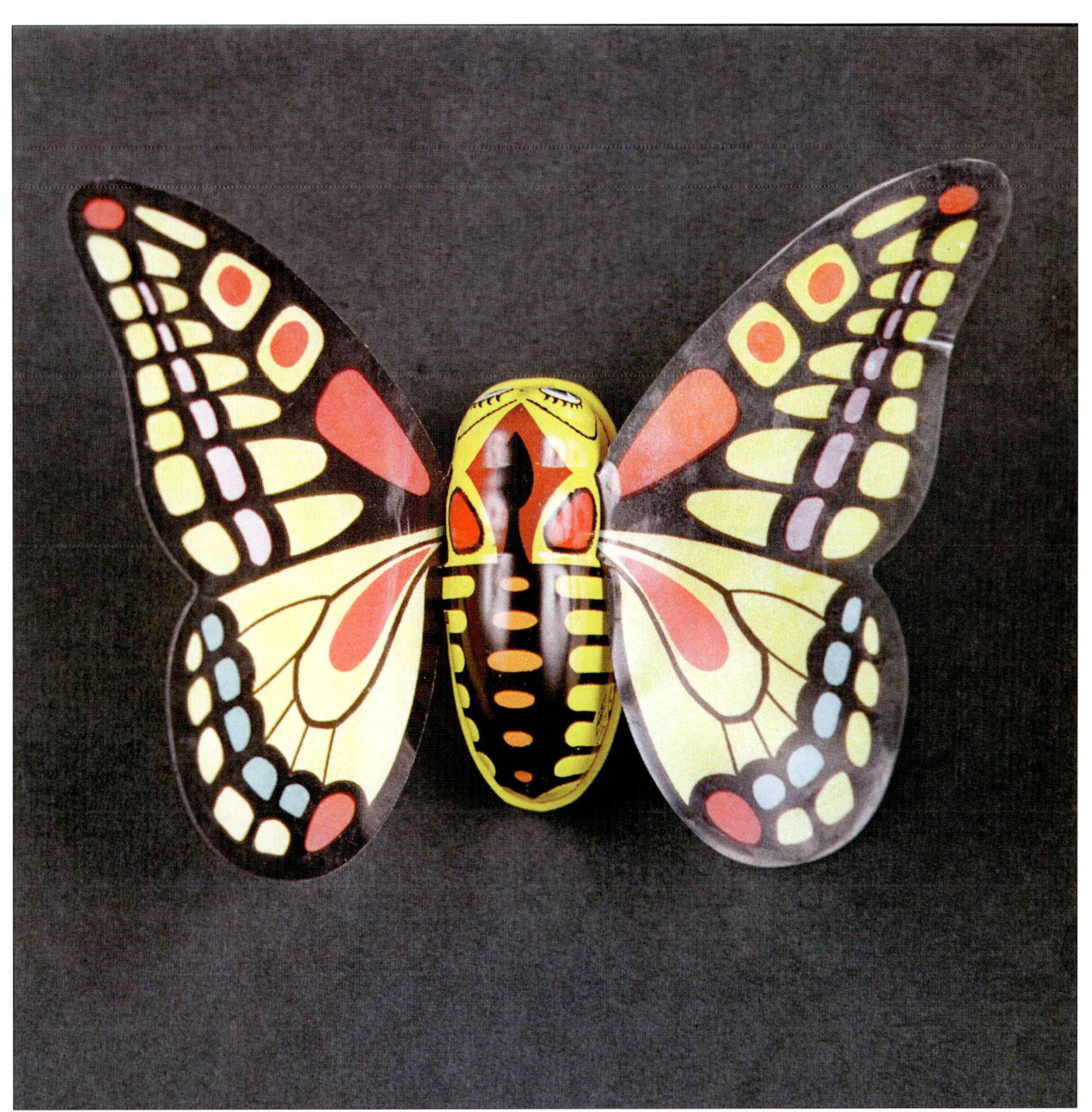

Plate 63

'Gibraltar' Pattern Service

Including plates, a Stamford teapot, a milk jug, a sandwich plate and a conical cup and saucer. Ceramics by Clarice Cliff, 1931. Private collection.

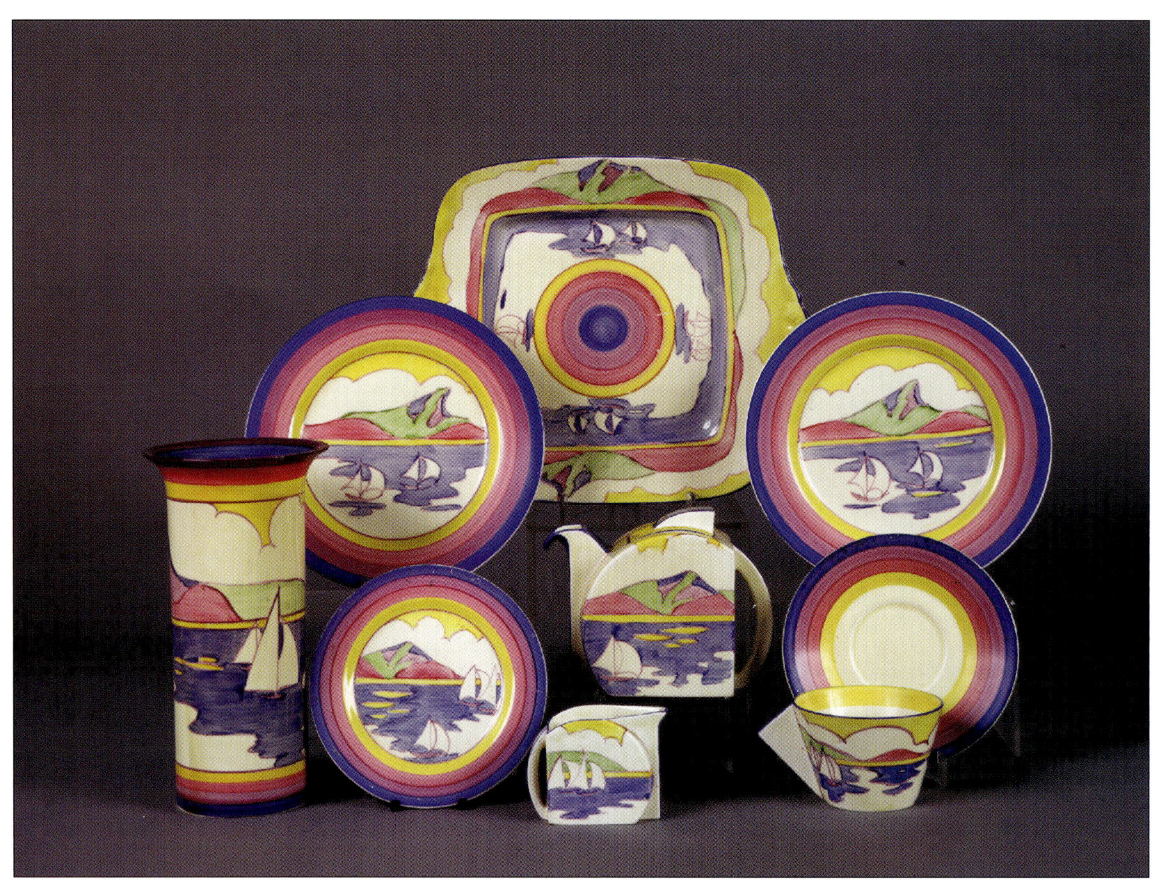

DUBONNET POSTER

Colour litho by Adolphe Jean Marie Cassandre, 1932. Private collection.

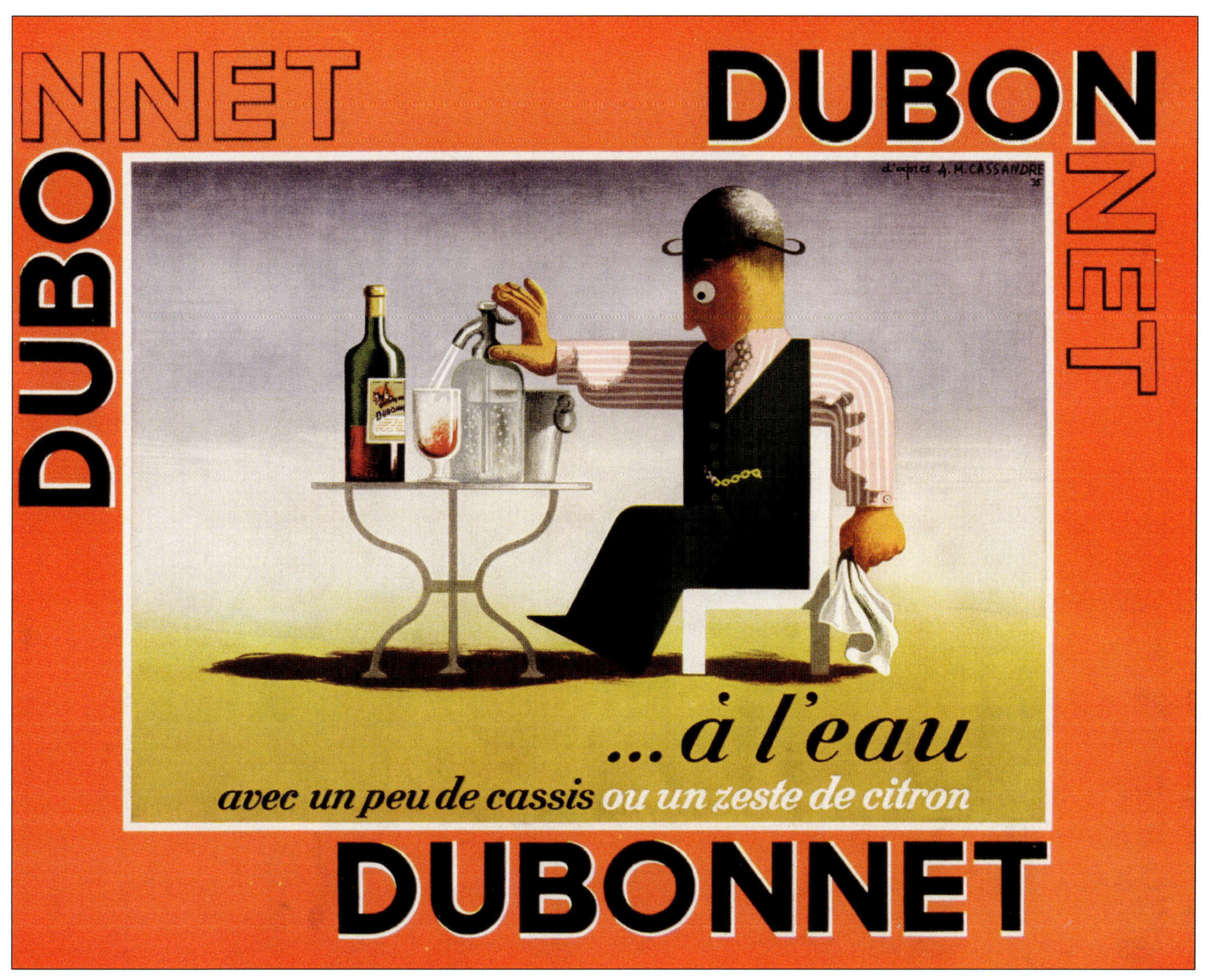

Plate 65

Entrance to the Hoover Building

Entrance to the Hoover Building, Western Avenue, Perivale, Middlesex
Designed by Wallis, Gilbert and Partner, 1932.

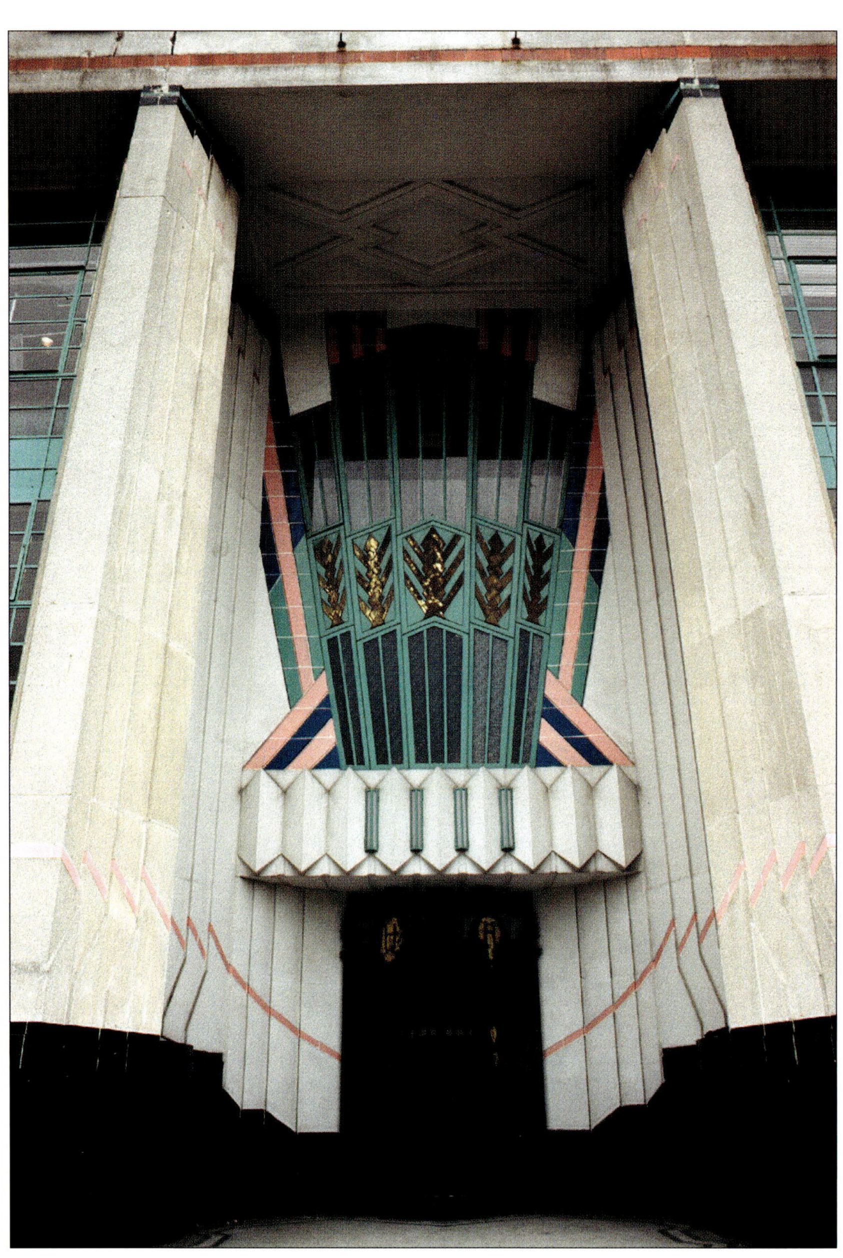

Allegorical Scene Depicting a Falcon and an Olive Branch

From the exterior of the Rockefeller Center, Manhattan, New York, by Lee Lawrie, c.1933.

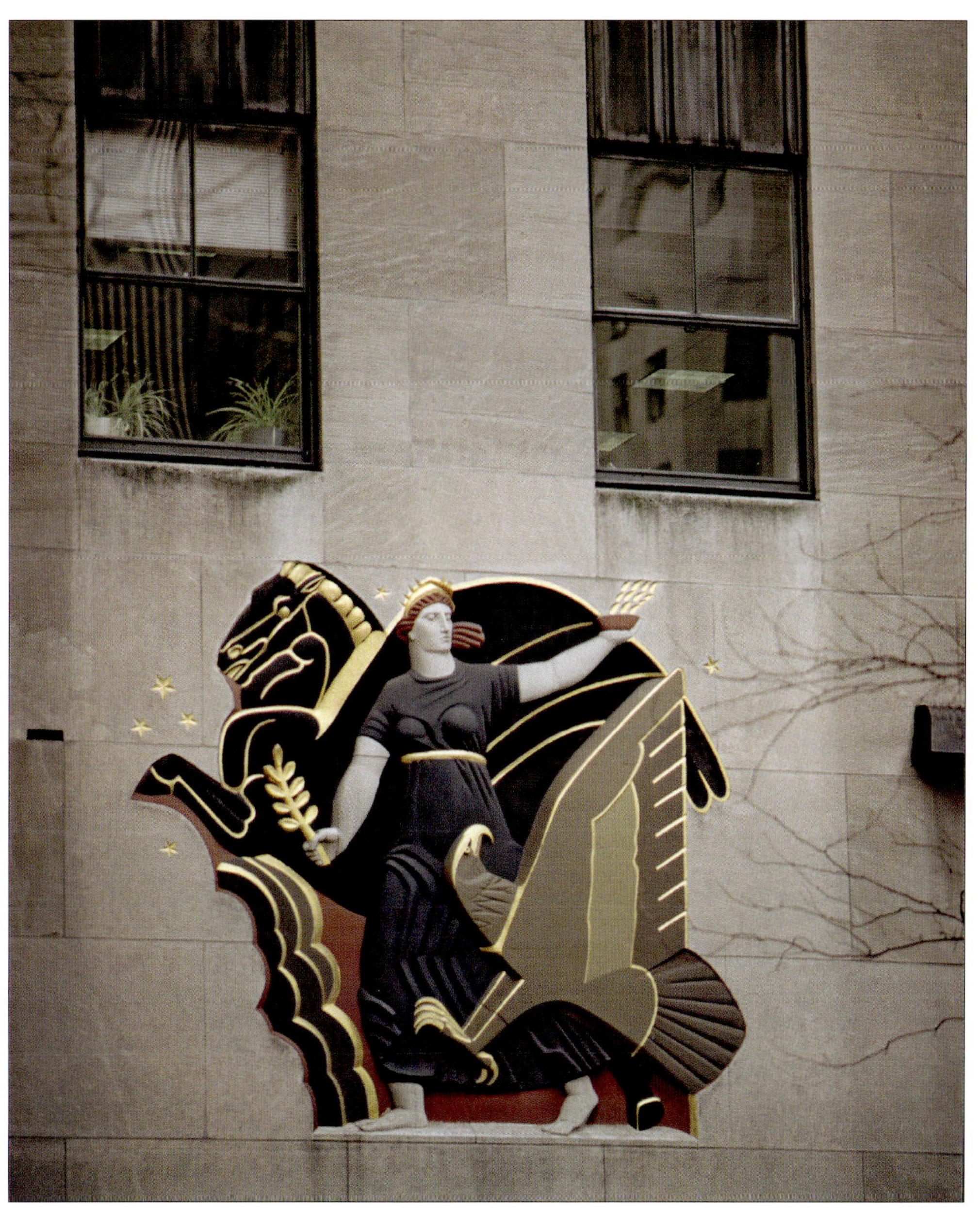

Plate 67

Bas-relief Depicting Mercury

Intaglio relief for the British Empire Building, Rockefeller Center, Manhattan, New York, by Lee Lawrie, 1933.

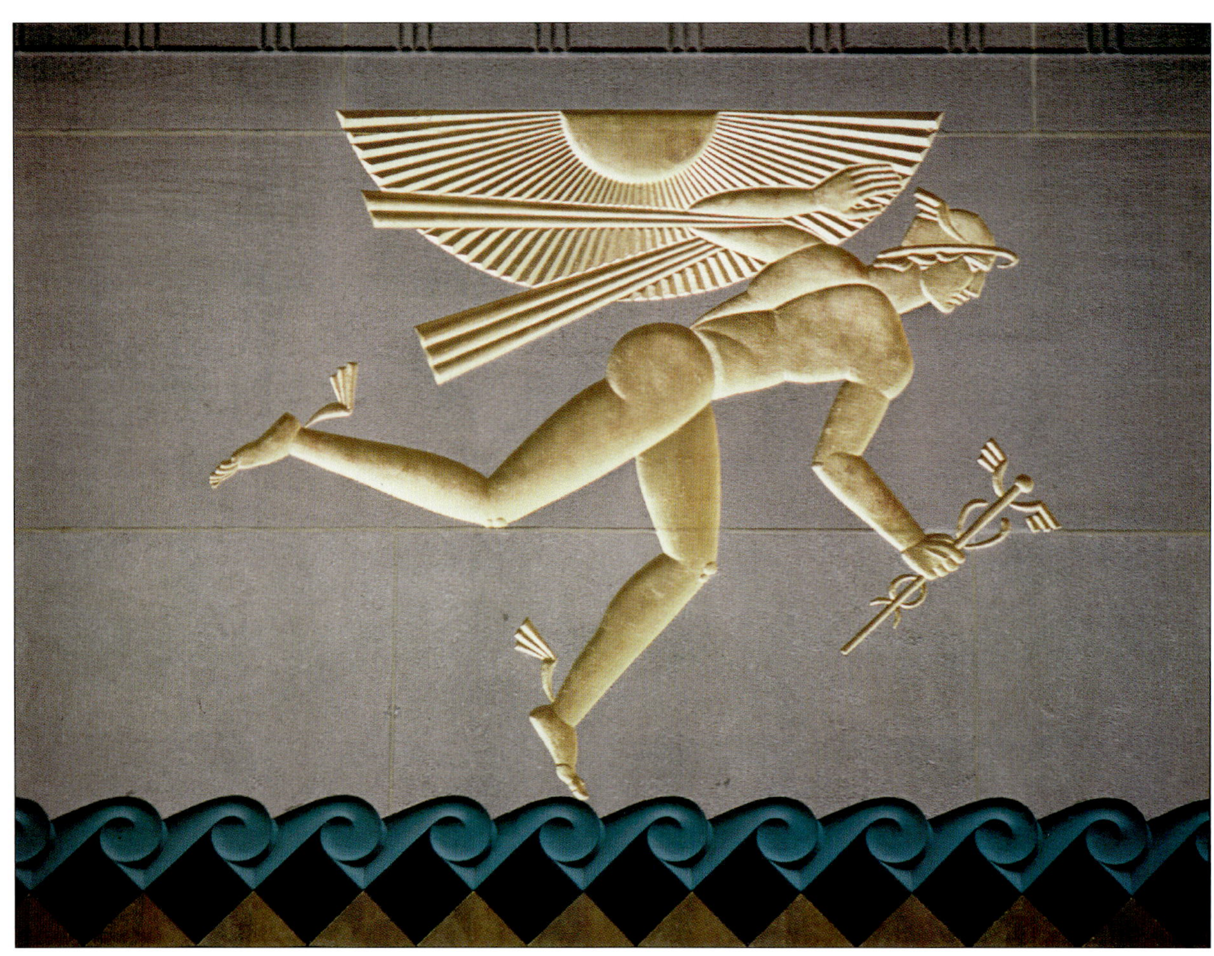

The Prometheus fountain

Plate 68

View of the Sunken Plaza and the RCA Building from the Channel Gardens.
Gilded bronze statue, by Paul Howard Manship, 1934.

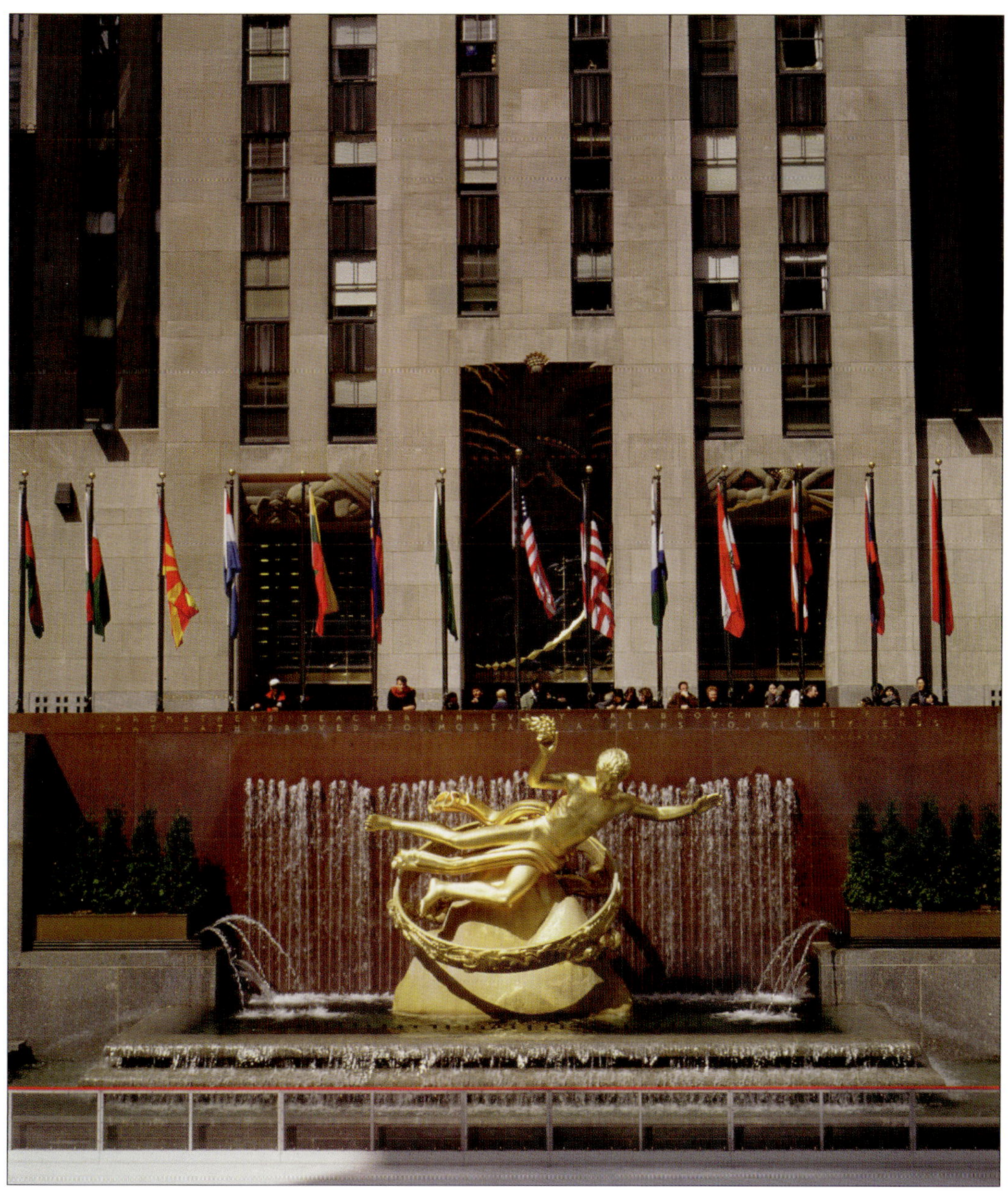

Plate 69

Vanity with Mirror

Chrome-plated tubular steel, wood and glass, by Kem Weber, manufactured by Lloyd Manufacturing Company, Menominee, Michigan, 1934. Brooklyn Museum of Art, New York, USA/ Modernism Benefit Fund.

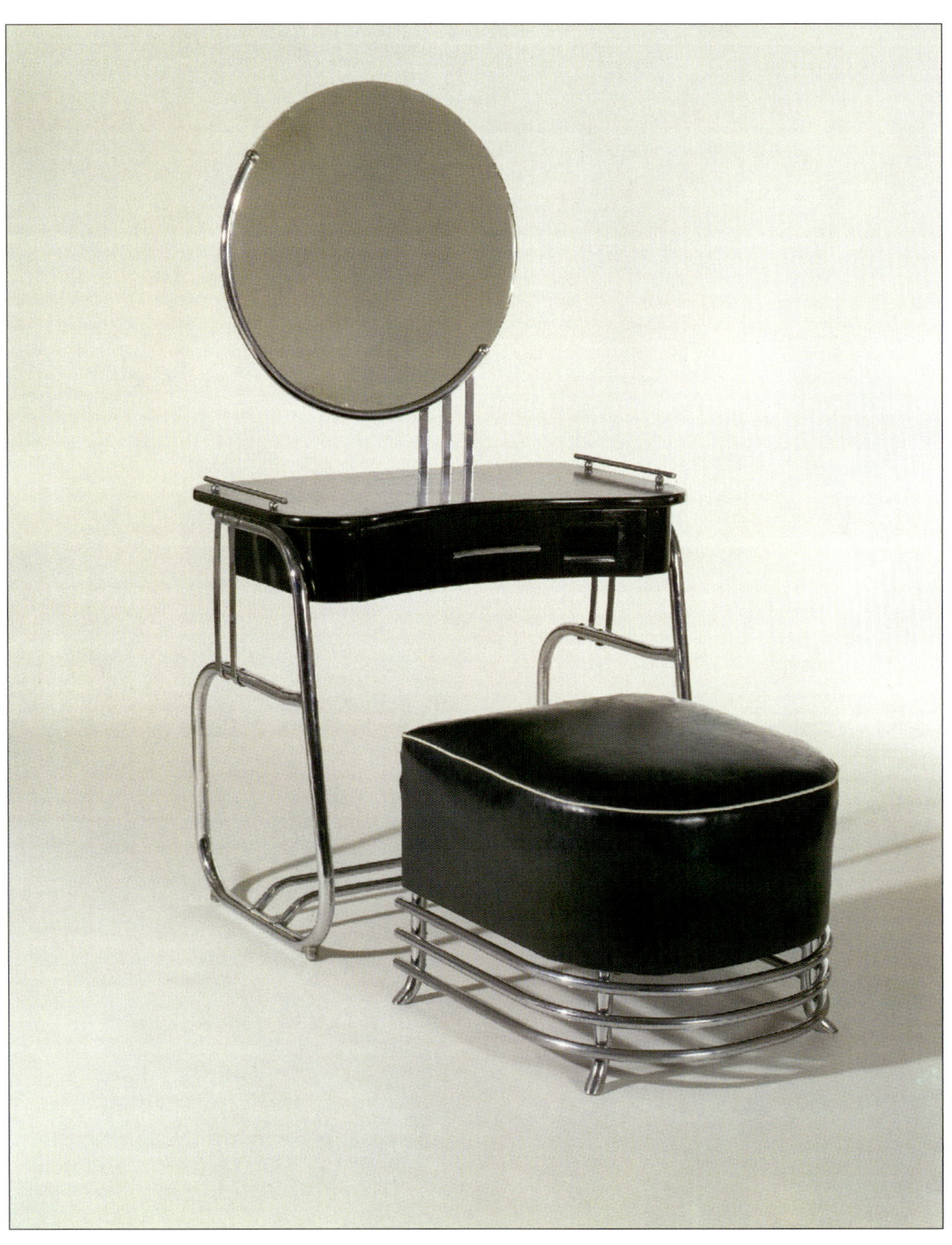

Poster Advertising Transatlantic Ferry Crossings *Plate 70*

Colour litho by Adolphe Jean-Marie Cassandre, printed by Alliance Graphique, Paris for Compagnie Generale Transatlantique, 1935. Private collection.

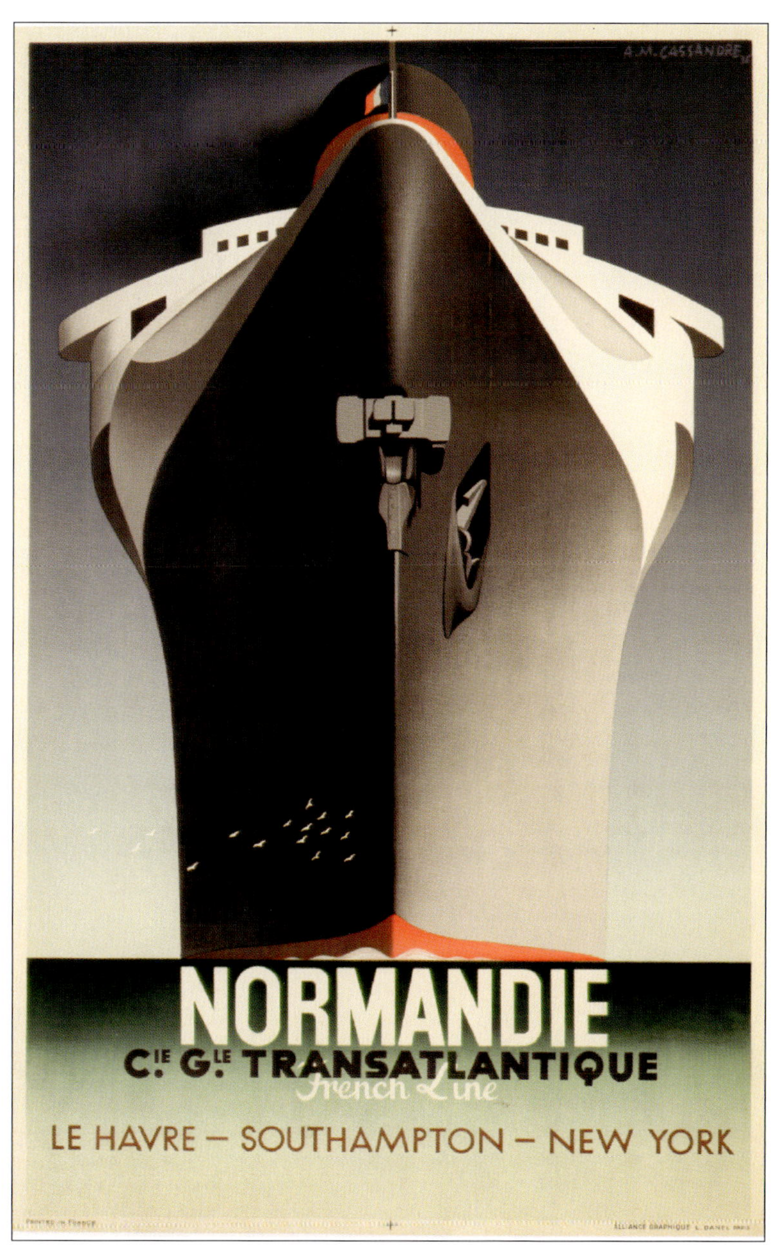

Plate 71

Great Salon on the 'Normandie'

View of the great salon of the SS Normandie, from L'illustration magazine, 1935. Private collection.

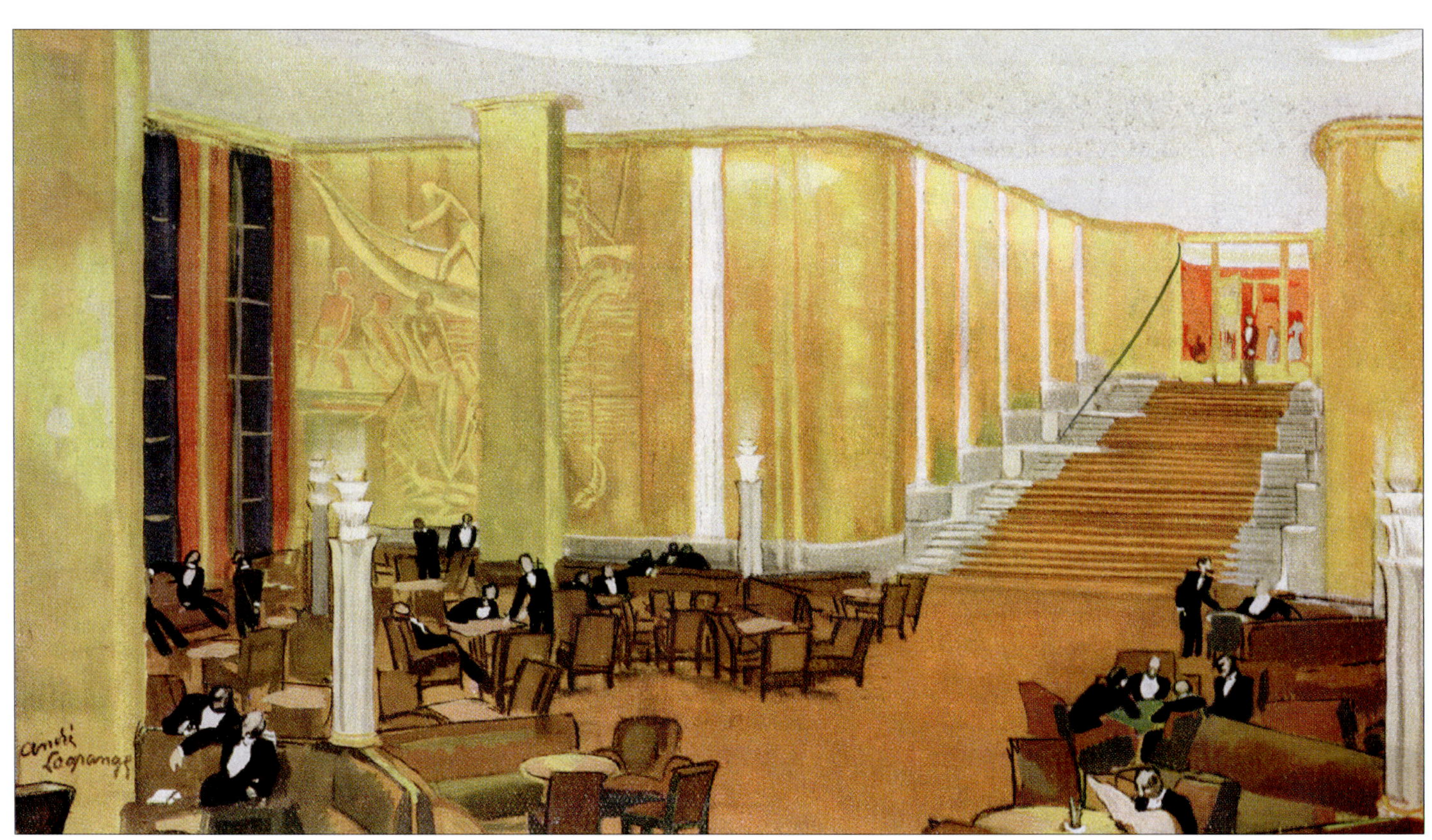

Chrome Table with Peach Mirror top

Plate 72

By an unknown artist, English school, c. 1935. Private collection.

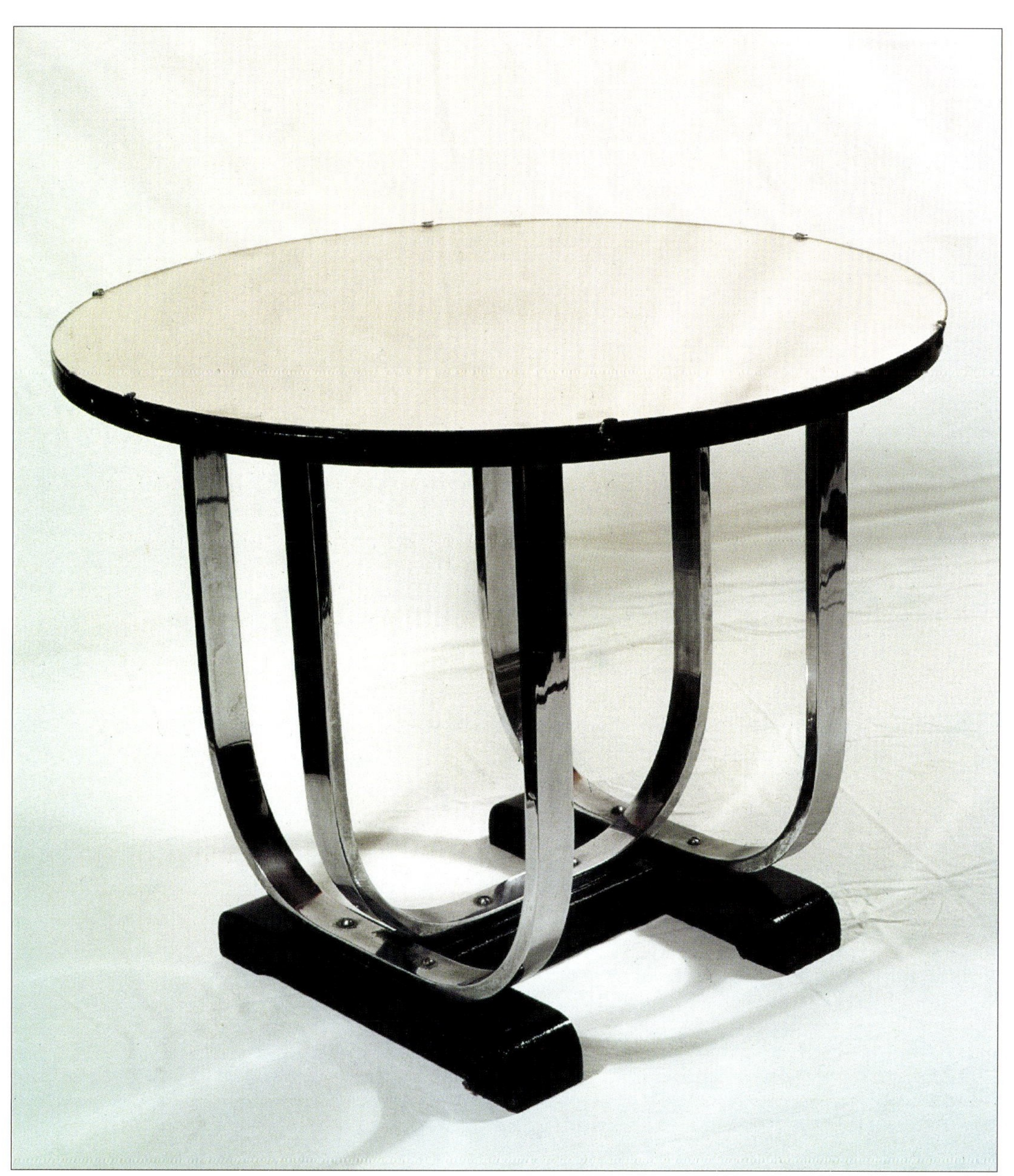

Plate 73

Teacup, Saucer and Plate

Earthenware, by Brexton, 1935. Photograph © Harris Museum and Art Gallery, Preston, Lancashire, UK.

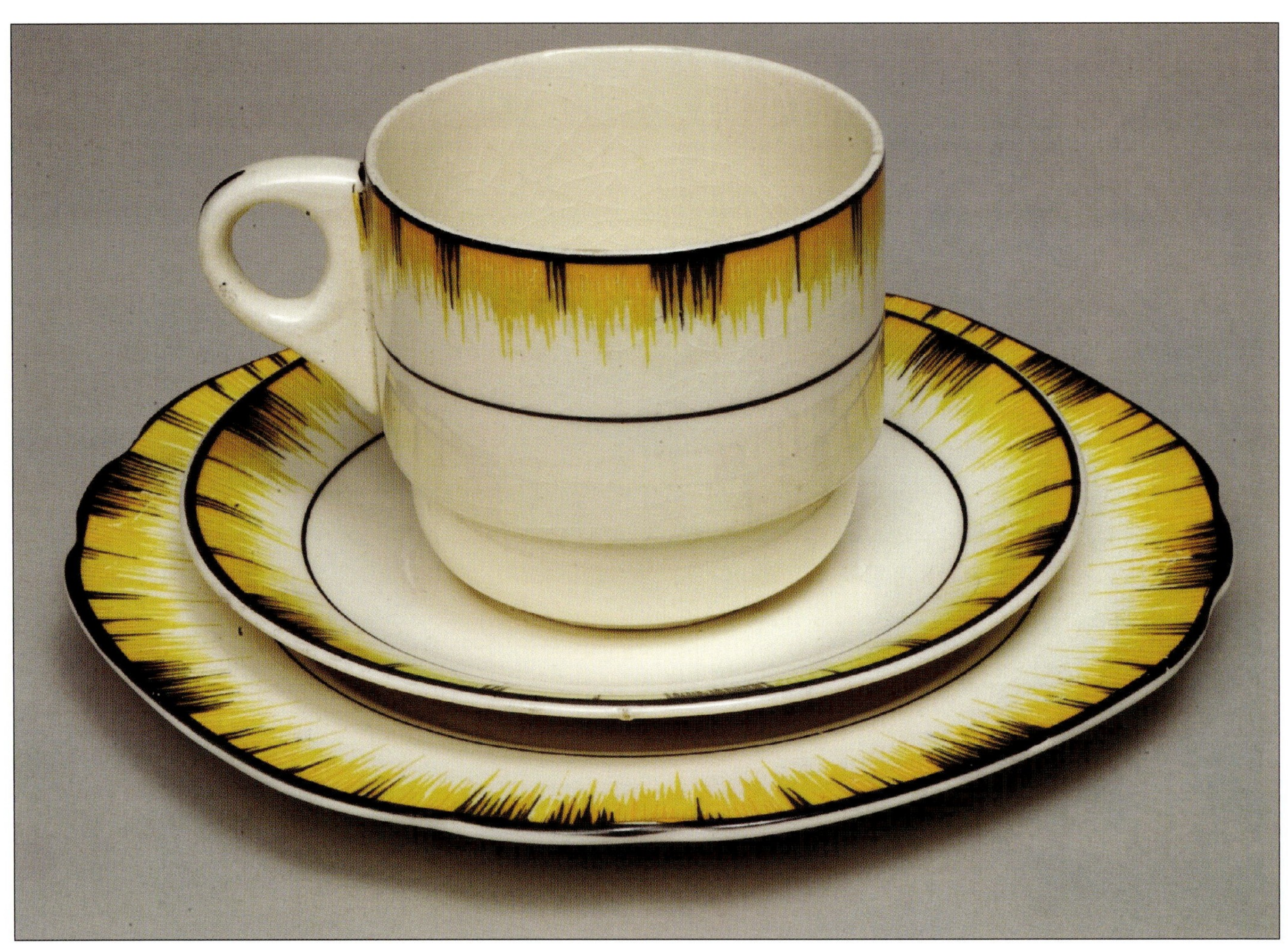

Kaufmann's Office

Plate 74

Kaufmann's Office, designed by Frank Lloyd Wright, 1935-37. Moved during the 1950s to the Victoria & Albert Museum, London, UK

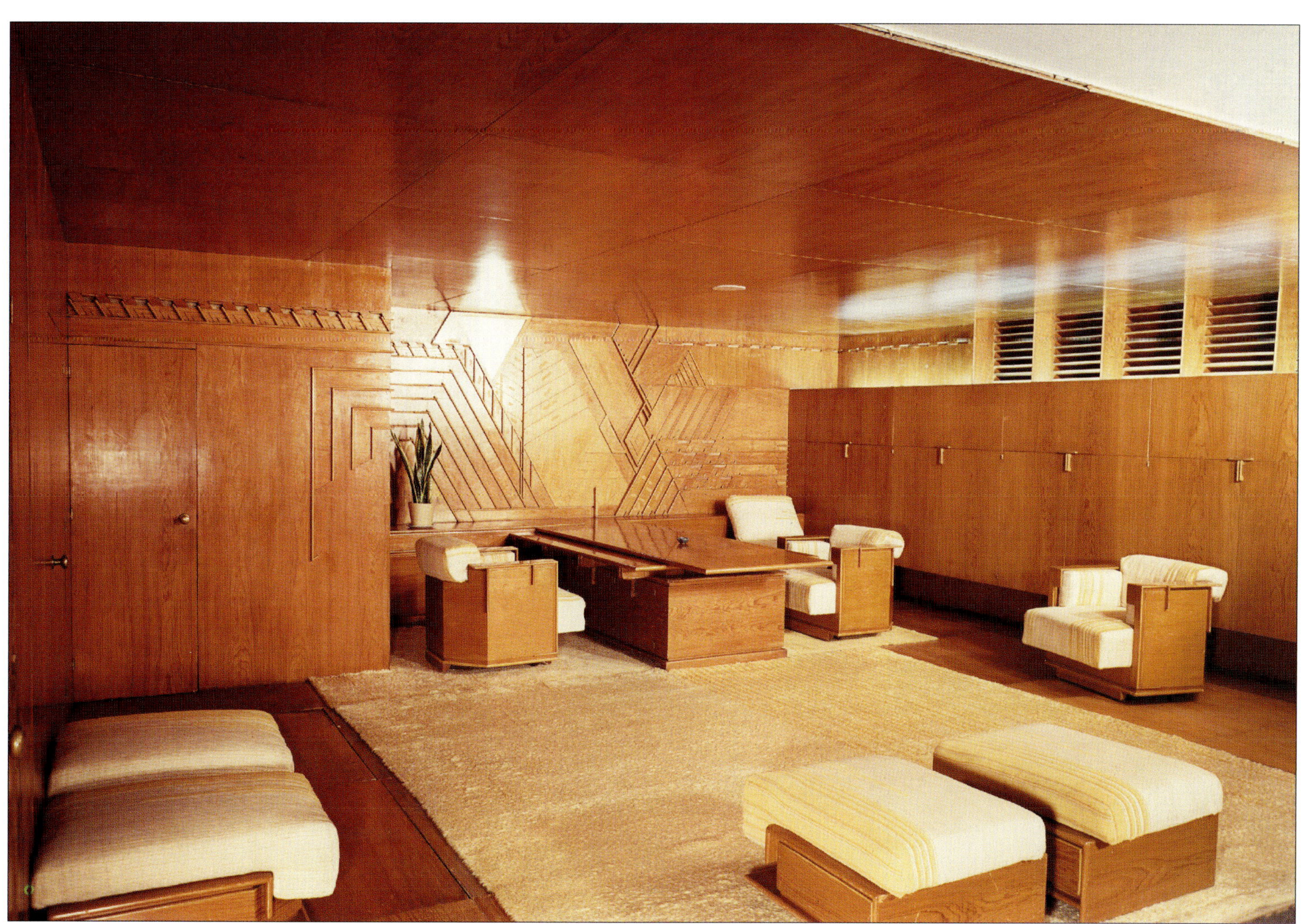

Plate 75

Breakwater Hotel, Miami Beach

Designed by Anton Skislewicz, c.1936-39.

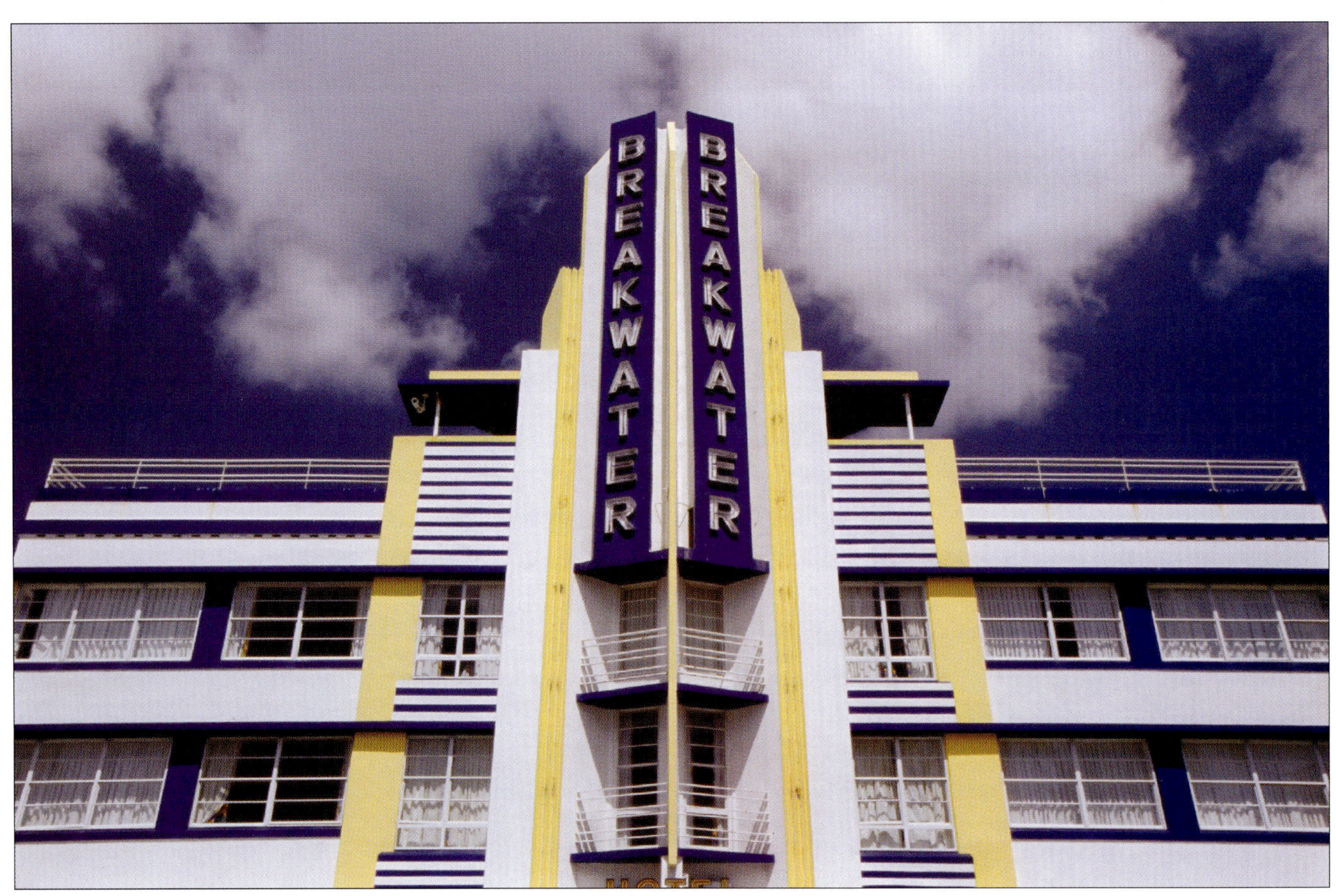

Modern Living Room

Modern Living Room, with formal subdued background, from 'Decorative Draperies and Upholstery', by E Thorne, 1937. Private collection/ The Stapleton Collection.

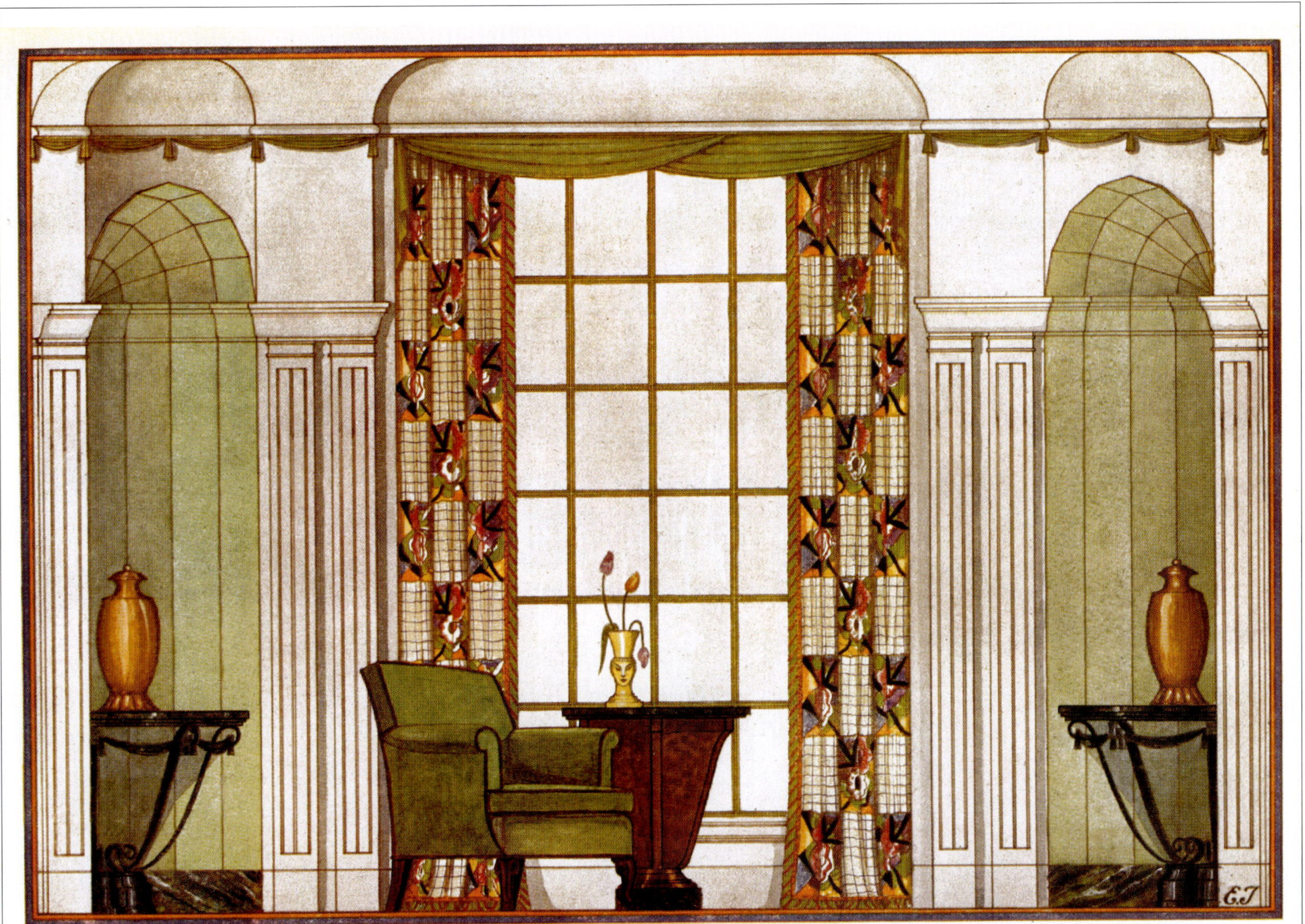

PLATE 2. MODERN LIVING ROOM WITH FORMAL SUBDUED BACKGROUND

Plate 77

'Falcon' Teapot

Ceramic teapot, by Susie Cooper for Crown Works, Burslem c.1930. Private Collection.

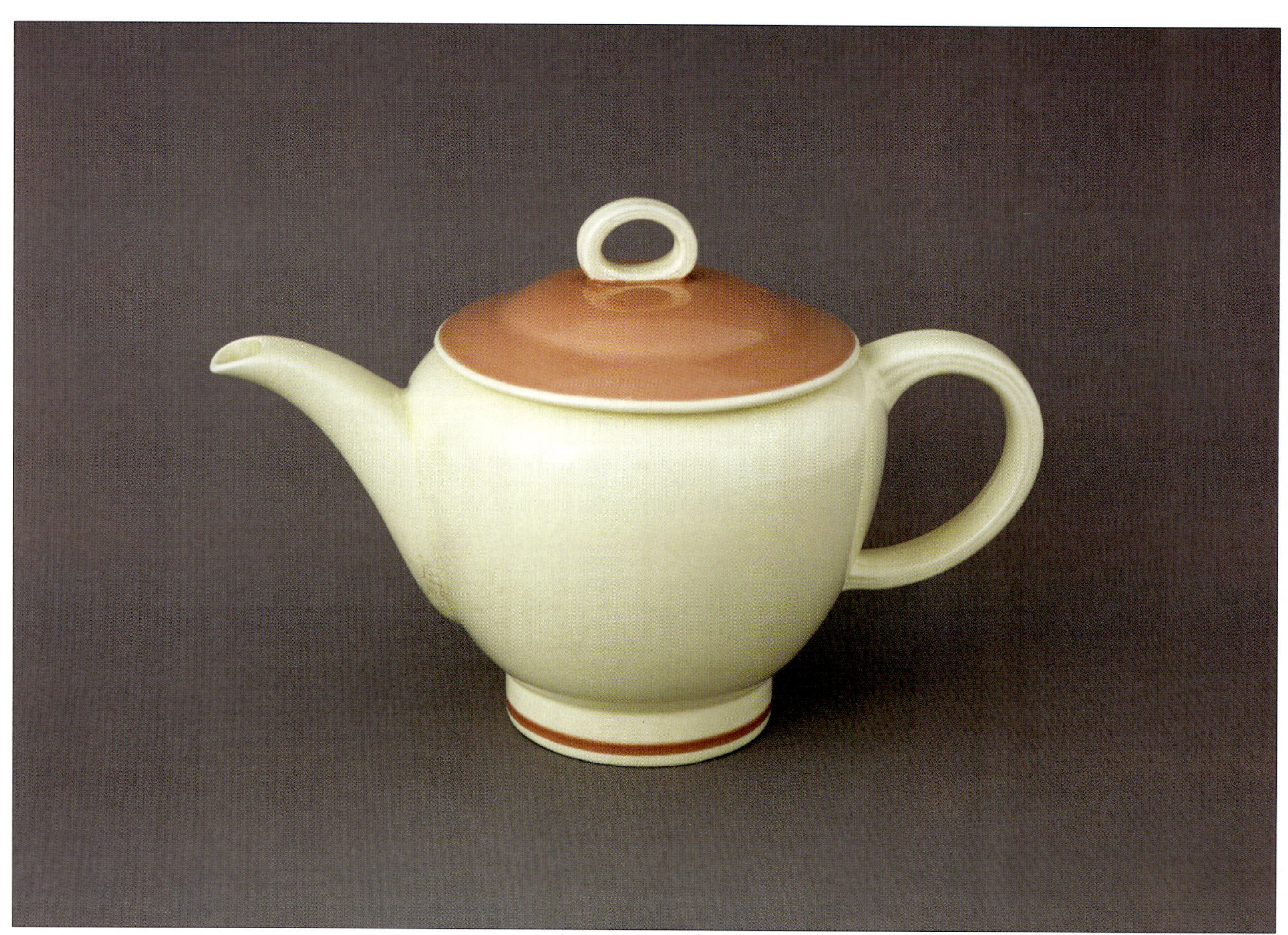

The Empire State Express

Plate 78

The 'Empire State Express' of the New York Central System in 1938. Photo by American Photographer (20th century). Private collection / Peter Newark American Pictures.

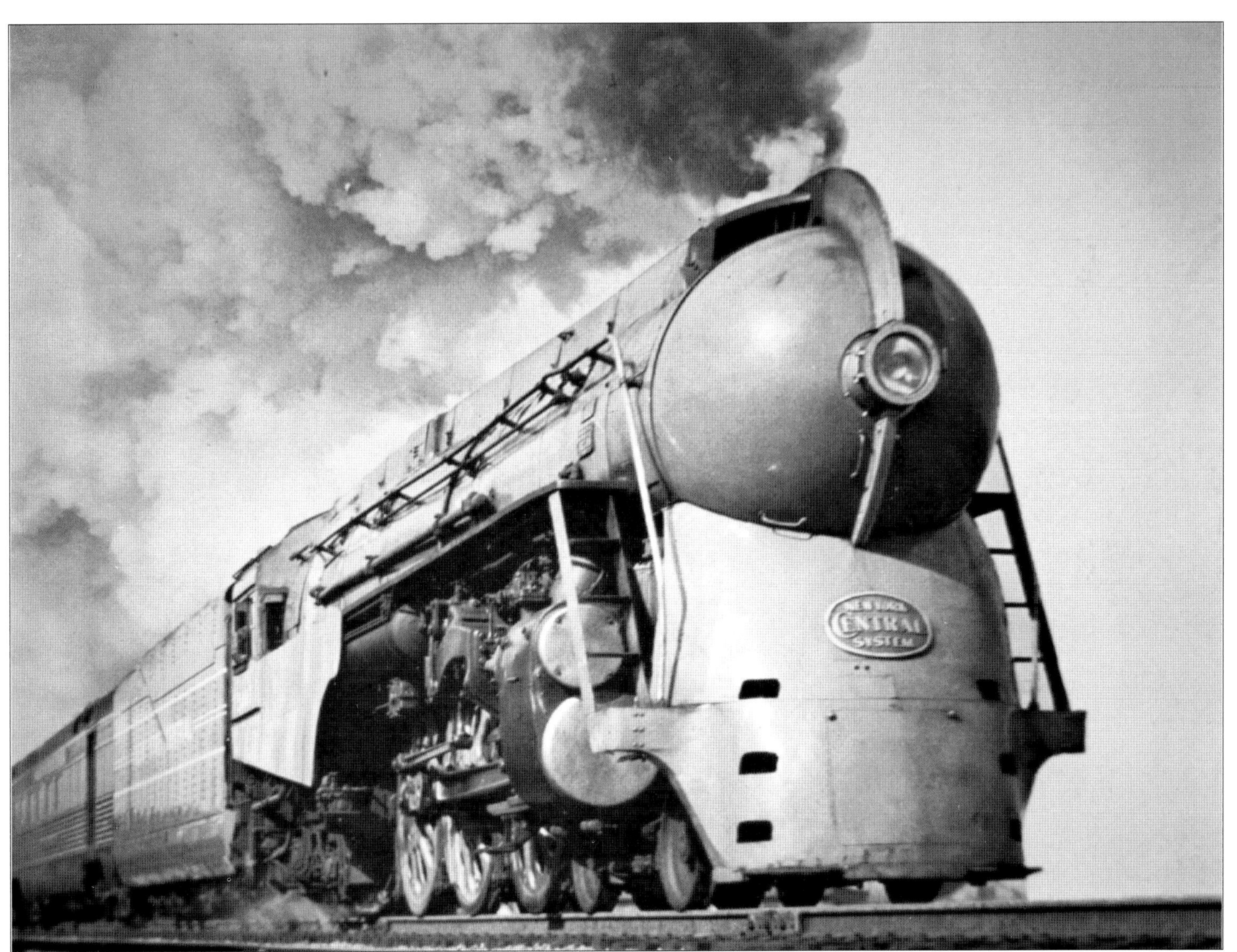

Plate 79

20TH CENTURY LIMITED

Poster advertising the new 16-hour train journey from New York to Chicago. Colour litho, by Leslie Ragan, 1938. Private collection.

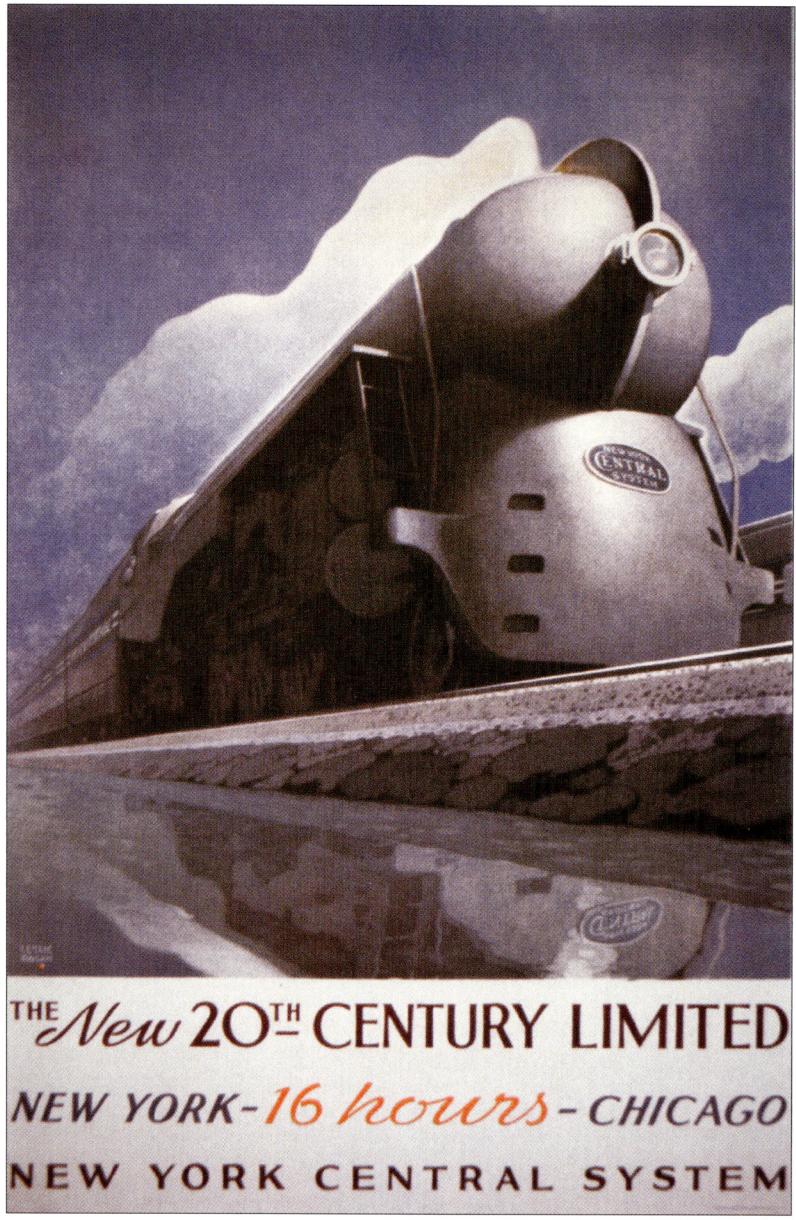

Star Cinema

Plate 80

Star Cinema, Glenthorpe Crescent, Leeds, Yorkshire, designed by James Brodie, c. 1938

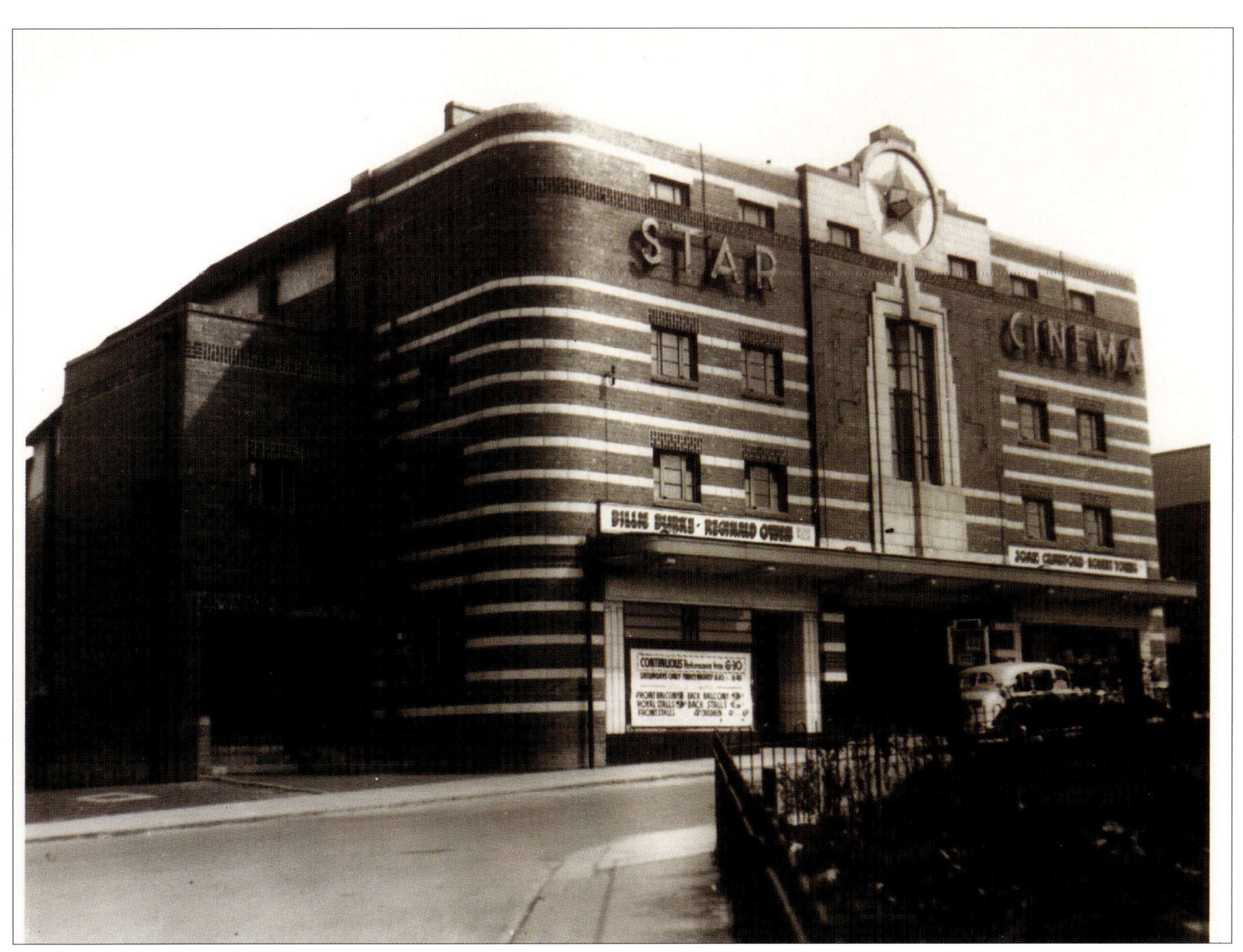

Plate 81

The Barber Institute of Fine Arts, Gallery Exterior

Designed by Robert Atkinson, c.1936–39

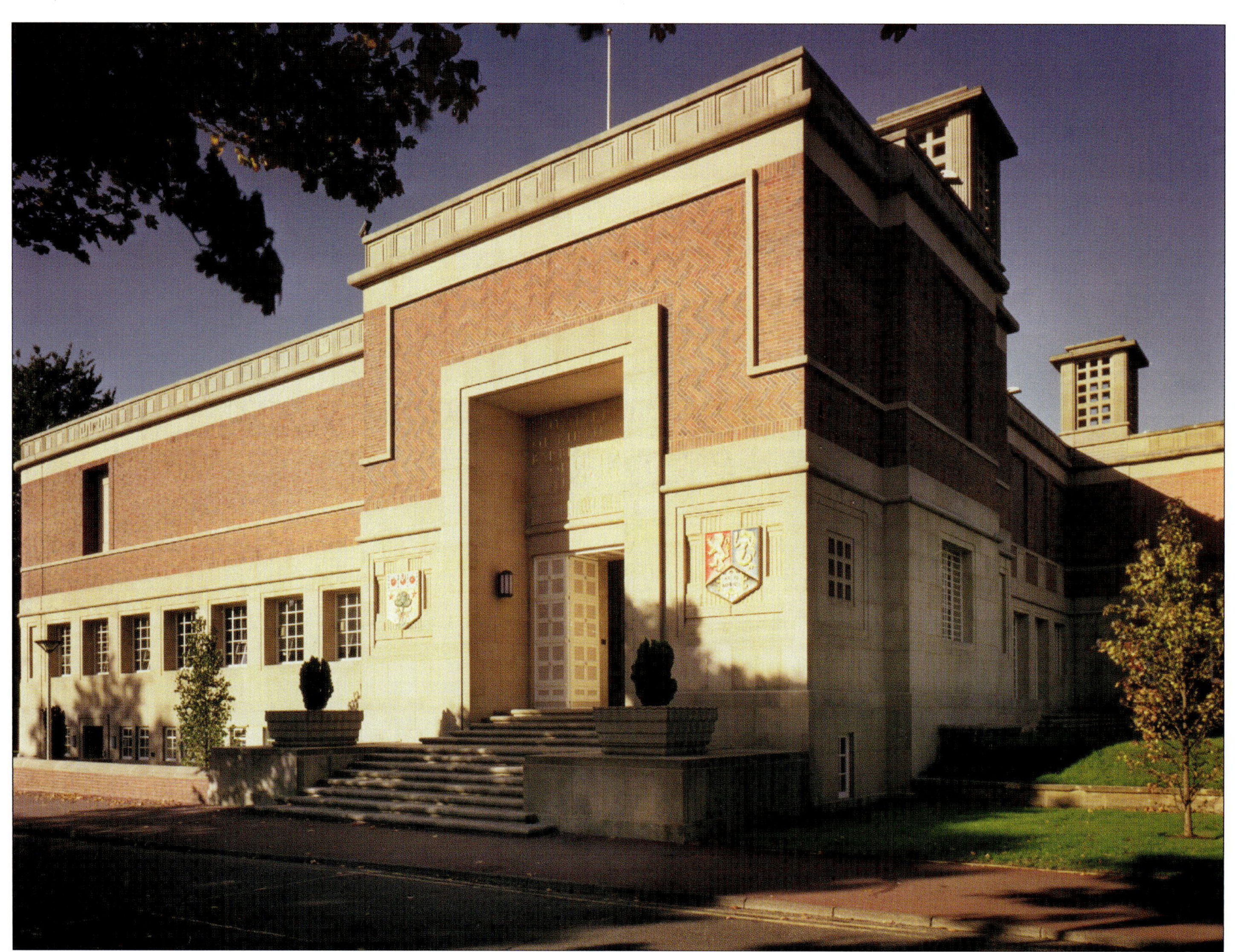

New York World's Fair, 1939

Plate 82

Trylon and Perisphere, or the Theme Centre, New York World's Fair, New York City, designed by architects Wallace Harrison and J. Andre Fouilhoux, 1939.

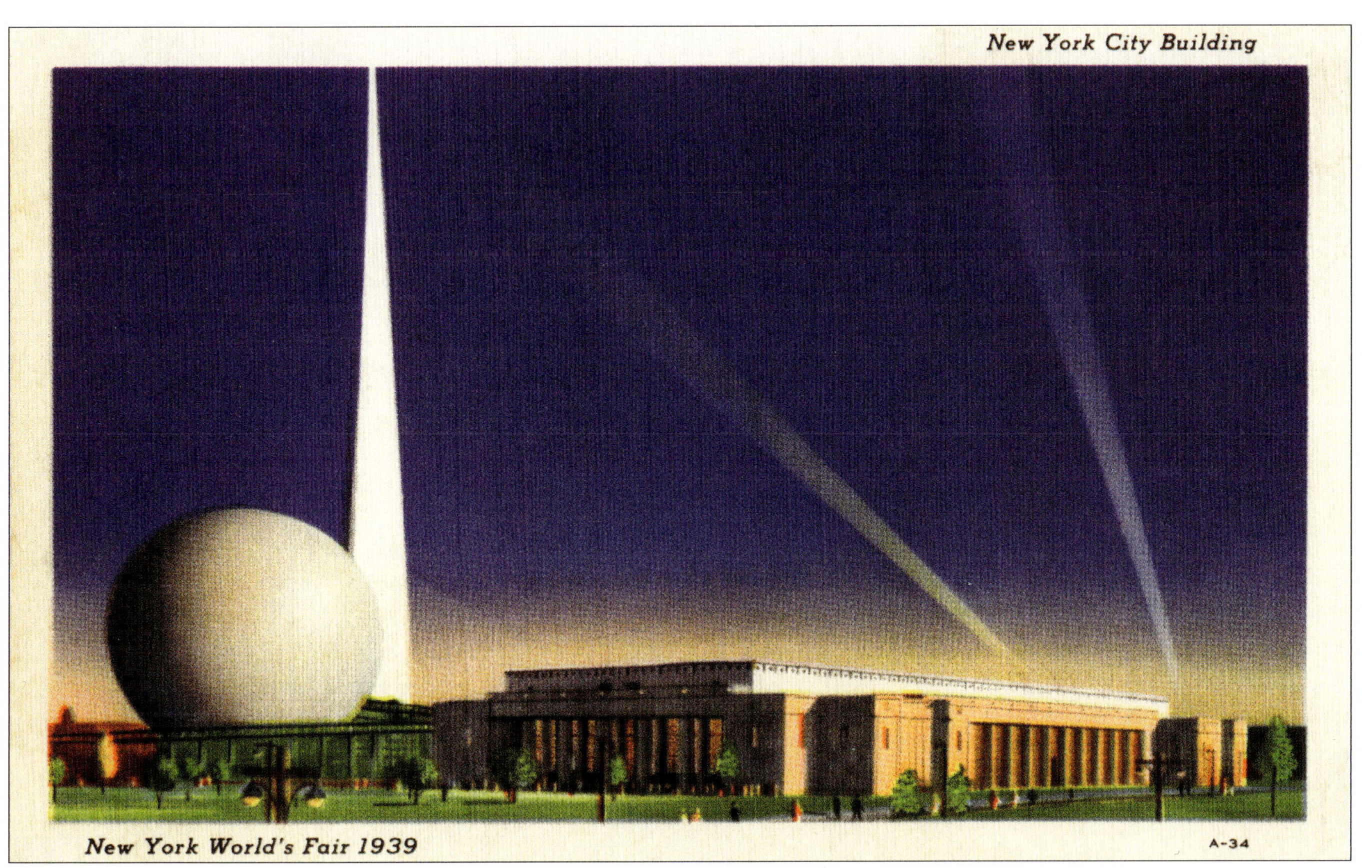

Alphabetical Index